HOW
TO AGE
without
GETTING
OLD

HOW TO AGE *without* GETTING OLD

THE STEPS YOU CAN TAKE TODAY TO STAY YOUNG FOR THE REST OF YOUR LIFE

JOYCE MEYER

Faith Words

New York • Nashville

FaithWords
Hachette Book Group
1290 Avenue of the Americas, New York, NY 10104
faithwords.com
twitter.com/faithwords

First Edition: March 2021

FaithWords is a division of Hachette Book Group, Inc.

The FaithWords name and logo are trademarks of Hachette Book Group, Inc.

The publisher is not responsible for websites (or their content) that are not owned by the publisher.

The Hachette Speakers Bureau provides a wide range of authors for speaking events. To find out more, go to www.hachettespeakersbureau.com or call (866) 376-6591.

Unless otherwise noted, Scripture quotations are taken from the Holy Bible, New International Version®, NIV®. Copyright ©1973, 1978, 1984, 2011 by Biblica, Inc.™ Used by permission of Zondervan. All rights reserved worldwide. www.zondervan.com The "NIV" and "New International Version" are trademarks registered in the United States Patent and Trademark Office by Biblica, Inc.™ | Scripture quotations marked AMPC are taken from the Amplified® Bible, Copyright © 1954, 1958, 1962, 1964, 1965, 1987 by The Lockman Foundation Used by permission. www.Lockman.org. | Scripture quotations marked ESV are taken from The Holy Bible, English Standard Version. ESV® Text Edition: 2016. Copyright © 2001 by Crossway Bibles, a publishing ministry of Good News Publishers. | Scripture quotations marked NLT are taken from the Holy Bible, New Living Translation, copyright ©1996, 2004, 2007, 2013, 2015 by Tyndale House Foundation. Used by permission of Tyndale House Publishers, Inc., Carol Stream, Illinois 60188. All rights reserved.

Library of Congress Cataloging-in-Publication Data

Names: Meyer, Joyce, 1943- author.
Title: How to age without getting old : the steps you can take today to stay young for the rest of your life / Joyce Meyer.
Description: First edition. | New York : FaithWords, 2021.
Identifiers: LCCN 2020042921 | ISBN 9781546026228 (hardcover) | ISBN 9781546029458 (large print) | ISBN 9781546026204 (ebook)
Subjects: LCSH: Aging--Religious aspects--Christianity. | Older Christians--Religious life.
Classification: LCC BV4580 .M475 2021 | DDC 248.8/5--dc23
LC record available at https://lccn.loc.gov/2020042921

Printed in the United States of America

LSC-C

Printing 1, 2021

CONTENTS

INTRODUCTION

Can you remember being very young and looking at someone in their fifties or sixties and saying, "She is *old*!" When we are in our teens or twenties, we cannot imagine being seventy-five years old. But eventually, we probably will be. The years pass for everyone. Some people navigate the changes associated with growing older gracefully, but many do not. Fearing, dreading, or refusing to admit that the aging process is happening doesn't eliminate it. Worrying about it or ignoring it certainly doesn't make aging any easier but, in fact, makes it more challenging.

I firmly believe that we should enjoy all the years that God gives us. In order to do so, we need to prepare for life's latter years. The earlier we begin this preparation, the easier it will be and the better the results will be.

During our young adult years and even into middle age, we are full of dreams and plans for the future. We're usually not thinking about getting older. Somehow, we mistakenly believe we will always be young. My youngest child just turned forty years old, and none of us can believe the baby of the family is forty! However, he

> *I firmly believe that we should enjoy all the years that God gives us.*

is, and he may find that being this age requires some minor changes and adjustments.

Not wanting to think about growing older is understandable, but problems arise when people are unwilling to make the changes each new season of life calls for and persist in being unwise in managing their health and their time. "Busy" is the disease of the twenty-first century, and it causes stress. If stress is ignored for too long, it will have long-term or even permanent negative effects on how we feel and what we are able to do as we grow older.

We can learn from the experiences of those who have gone before us, and I hope this book will provide some lessons from my life for you. My goal in these pages is to share openly the experiences and knowledge I have gained over the years in regard to aging. My hope is that it will help you avoid some of the mistakes I have made so that you can age well.

> *I would like you to say aloud right now, "I will not fear or dread the years ahead."*

We can do nothing about adding one year to our age every twelve months, but there is *a lot* we can do to keep from "getting old."

I would like you to say aloud right now, "Someday I am going to be seventy-five years old, and then eighty and perhaps ninety, depending on how many years God gives me. I will not fear or dread the years ahead."

No matter how young you are right now, I think it is important to think about your latter years. Let me encourage you to look forward to them and believe that even though life will be different when you are older, it can still be very, very good.

You may notice as you read that I have not filled this book with pages of statistics on aging. You can access those easily by searching the Internet if you are interested in them. I have found some of them to be very negative. I don't want to expect my body and mind to break down at a certain age because that's what the experts predict. I want to see what God does with me. I believe that He has an individual plan for each of us and for the course of our lives. If we follow His guidance, we will end up at the right place at the right time.

> *I don't want to expect my body and mind to break down at a certain age because that's what the experts predict. I want to see what God does with me.*

Before you read further, let me challenge you to ask yourself an important question: Will you simply let yourself "get old," or will you age gracefully, purposefully, and wisely, allowing God to use you in every season of your life? If you will, I believe your latter years can be absolutely wonderful.

"Keys to joy at any age:
Live simply.
Give generously.
Receive graciously.
Stay grateful."

—

P.C.F.

CHAPTER 1

LEARNING FROM EXPERIENCE, PART 1

There's a beauty and wisdom to experience that cannot be faked.

Amy Grant

If I were to ask you to share your life experiences with me, how would the conversation unfold? Would you tell me stories of a happy childhood, recount your dreams and disappointments, or show me photos of your family? Would you reminisce about the challenges you've overcome and the lessons you've learned? Would I hear you speak about your life with gratitude for all that God has done for you? Would I perceive fear or anxiety about the days to come, or would I hear peace, faith, and positivity in your attitude toward the future? Everyone's life experience is different, and God can use it all. In this chapter and the next one, I'd like to share some of the experiences that have led me to write this book.

A LONG JOURNEY BEGINS

I was abused sexually by my father on a regular basis through-out my childhood and teenage years. I am sure that the stress of that experience stole a lot of my energy before I ever had a chance to use it properly. For years, I thought that my being strong and determined got me through those terrible years of abuse, but I now realize it was God who gave me the strength to keep going.

I can remember not feeling well at different times through-out my life, beginning at about age eighteen. I left home as soon as I was legally old enough to do so, and I married at age eighteen—interestingly, the same year I began facing chal-lenges with my health. There's no way to characterize my first marriage except to say that it was bad and extremely stressful. On two occasions, my husband abandoned me. I also had to deal with his many extramarital affairs, his lack of employ-ment, and his habit of stealing.

I soon found myself going to doctors, asking why I did not feel well so much of the time. They tried to tell me that my physical symptoms were stress related, but I refused to accept "stress" as a real diagnosis. The reason that any men-tion of stress, nerves, or an emotional connection to the way I felt physically was unacceptable to me is that my mother had trouble with anxiety throughout her life and finally experi-enced a nervous breakdown. I thought being susceptible to stress meant that I was weak and could not handle life, and I did not want anyone to view me that way.

I now suspect that excessive stress is the culprit behind

many health problems. I have personally experienced stress-related health conditions and have known other people who have experienced them, too. I will elaborate on the connection between stress and health throughout this book, but for now, let me simply say that the symptoms of many illnesses are real, but their root cause—or at least a strong contributor to many of them—is stress.

After getting a divorce at the age of twenty-two, I was alone in the world with my first child. With no one to turn

> *I now suspect that excessive stress is the culprit behind many health problems.*

to for help, I lived in a constant state of low-level fear and worry. I could ask my father for help, but I knew that would mean suffering more abuse, so I avoided it as long as I possibly could. I finally did have to move back home for a short period of time, during which I met and married Dave. He was and always has been a patient and loving man, but I was so dysfunctional and my soul was so wounded because of my past that I didn't know how to enjoy Dave or anything else in life. I didn't realize that all the stress I had been through had taken a toll on my body. Yet because I was still young and had the energy that young people enjoy, I pressed on, despite dealing with increasing physical issues.

BUSIER AND BUSIER

When Dave and I married, he adopted my son, David, and we quickly had two more babies, both girls. Within a few years, we had three children all under six years old, lived in a small apartment that consisted of three rooms, and had barely enough money to get by. When we decided we wanted to buy our first home, I had to get a job to make the purchase possible, so I added the stress of working full-time on top of trying to do everything else the life of a young wife and mother required. I drank way too much coffee, smoked a pack of cigarettes a day, slept about six hours a night, and was upset about something most of the time. Although I didn't know it at the time, I also had a birth defect in my right hip. My hip joint was oblong instead of round, so it didn't fit properly and caused me back problems that started when I was a teenager. Thankfully, that was eventually taken care of through a hip replacement, but not until 2017. From my teenage years until my early seventies, I had back pain and was constantly going to the chiropractor for adjustments.

Although I had believed in Jesus since I was a child, I lacked a real relationship with Him for many years. But in 1976, when I was thirty-three years old, this began to change. God drew me to Himself and gave me a love and passion for studying His Word. As a result, I began to realize that I needed a lot of change in my life in order to solve the problems with which I struggled. Over a period of many years, while I received a lot of healing from Him in my soul and aspects of my life got better, I still didn't know how to rest. I could barely speak the words *I can't*. I had deep insecurities, and I thought my worth and value came from what I produced through hard work, so most of the time I worked.

By the time I was thirty-six, Dave and I had our fourth

child, and God had called us into ministry. Starting anything new is usually a lot of hard work, and ministry is no different. We started with nothing, and over a forty-year period, by God's grace, we have built an international ministry that reaches around the world via television, other media, books, conferences, and speaking engagements.

As both my family and the ministry grew, I constantly worked not only physically but also internally, by worrying, planning, thinking, reasoning, and pondering the teachings I prepared. Most of us can live that way for a period of time, but sooner or later it catches up with us, and life gets harder and harder. I recall the first time I got really sick. I had no energy for anything, but through eating healthily and making a few changes in my lifestyle, I recovered fairly quickly. However, I didn't learn anything from the experience, so I simply kept doing what I had always done and eventually got sick again. We cannot keep doing the same thing over and over and expect to get different results.

> *We cannot keep doing the same thing over and over and expect to get different results.*

HEADACHES AND HORMONES

When I was in my forties, I began having migraine headaches associated with hormonal changes, and they lasted for about ten years. Some experts say that unbalanced hormones cause stress, and others say that stress causes unbalanced hormones. Either way, stress is something we must recognize and deal with. In my opinion, excessive stress is a cause of unbalanced hormones—or if it is not *the* cause, at the very least it magnifies the problem.

It is very important for a woman to be in good health when she enters into the change of life. For most women, this happens between the ages of forty-five and fifty-five, but it begins in some women as early as their thirties or forties and in some as late as sixty. I have noticed just from watching my friends that some women have no problems at all with the change. They simply stop having their periods and go on with life. But others have many problems. Hot flashes, weight gain, night sweats, sleep disturbances, mood changes, irritability, headaches, and simply not feeling well are all common symptoms. Why do some go through the change so easily while others suffer quite a bit? I think part of the reason lies in the condition of their general health when the change of life hits and how much stress they live under.

> *Why do some go through the change so easily while others suffer quite a bit?*

I had a very difficult time with the change of life because I was already depleted of energy and nutrition when it began. I was also under a lot of stress from my past and the hard work required in beginning the ministry. I have an adrenal adenoma or adrenal dysplasia (the adrenal glands control the hormones in our bodies). This means I have a small, noncancerous growth on my left adrenal gland. Doctors have advised me not to have it removed because of the danger of doing so. I have read that some physicians say an adrenal adenoma causes no problems at all, but my doctor believes that it does affect the release of hormones in my body and has caused some of the problems I have experienced.

I have a strong personality and lots of determination, so although I didn't always feel good, I pressed on. One doctor told me that my mind was stronger than my body, meaning that no matter how bad I felt or how tired I was, I had the ability just to keep going.

The only way I know to describe how I felt during those years is that I couldn't relax, I struggled often with those terrible headaches, and I was exhausted. Once again, the doctor said it was stress, but I refused to take any medicine that might

> *My mind was stronger than my body.*

help me. After all, I was strong in the Lord and believed in His healing power, so I kept pushing.

TWO HEALTH CRISES WITHIN FIVE YEARS

In 1980, I had a hysterectomy because of excessive bleeding and pain. In approximately 1985, I had a regular breast checkup as part of an annual doctor's visit, and to my utter surprise I found out I had a cancerous tumor. Thankfully, the mass was small. However, it was a fast-growing, estrogen-dependent tumor, so I needed a mastectomy because surgery was the preferred treatment at the time. Because my lymph nodes were clear, I didn't have to have radiation or chemotherapy, for which I was and am still extremely thankful. Each year when I hear that my mammogram is clear, I am very grateful. More than thirty years have passed since that particular health challenge, and I thank God for every one of them.

The hysterectomy caused me to enter the change of life early. Due to the breast cancer, I could not take hormones to help with the discomfort of menopause, and I had a very difficult time with it. But during these health challenges, I never stopped long enough to let my body rest or heal properly. I tried to relax when I wasn't doing conferences, but even when I sat in a chair or lay down to rest, I stayed busy internally. I never allowed my soul (my mind, will, and emotions) to rest. I was always thinking, planning, worrying, and trying to make decisions.

> *I never allowed my soul to rest. I was always thinking, planning, worrying, and trying to make decisions.*

By that time, the ministry had grown larger, and we had even opened offices in several countries outside the United States because of our broad television outreach. We employed approximately nine hundred people, who needed and expected paychecks, and I saw no option but to keep going because our income depended on my speaking schedule. At least I thought it did. My schedule during that season was so full that I was rarely home for more than a few days. I had waited so long for opportunities to teach God's Word that I viewed each one as a door God had opened for me.

While it is true that God does open doors of opportunity

for us, it is also true that every door that opens isn't necessarily one that He wants us to walk through. We are to use wisdom regarding what we agree to do or choose not to do. In my book *In Search of Wisdom*, I mention a specific way one of my friends uses wisdom concerning her commitments:

I once asked a friend in ministry how she decided which speaking invitations to accept and which to decline. She told me that before she responded to an invitation, she thought through every detail of what it would take for her to do it. She thought about matters such as how long she would be away from home, what kind of preparation time she would need to invest, and how far she would have to travel. Although these are all logistical questions and not ministry-related ones, she was wise to ask them. If we do not ask wise questions, we may agree to do something and then later complain about it and dread doing it because we did not consider the details involved in it. It is always better to pray and think about a commitment before giving an answer.

> *While it is true that God does open doors of opportunity for us, it is also true that every door that opens isn't necessarily one that He wants us to walk through.*

I wish I had known what my friend knew during those days when my schedule was so packed. I stayed extremely busy—too busy, in fact—because I had not yet learned to say no. People who cannot say no when needed will usually end up with overloaded calendars and experience the effects of stress. The main reason many people overcommit is that they want to please others, but we must be God-pleasers, not people-pleasers.

During those years, I didn't feel bad all the time, but certainly more than I should have. I loved teaching God's Word, and I still do. I was full of dreams and visions for the future and very passionate about everything I did. When we are passionate about something, that passion gives us the determination to do whatever needs to be done in order to accomplish it. My joy in being able to teach God's Word and help people was greater than any physical discomfort, so I generally ignored the way I felt.

> We must be God-pleasers, not people-pleasers.

Maybe you can relate to my story in many ways. I am sharing openly with you about my life behind the scenes so that, if you feel the same, you will know that you are not alone and that you too can find answers and live an enjoyable, fruitful life.

"I would encourage younger people to remember these things as they age:

- Make time with God a daily priority.
- Take good care of your body and love yourself the way God made you.
- Learn to laugh at yourself.
- Pray always, turning things over to God and trusting Him.
- Slow down and take time for the little things, because the days pass quickly.
- Make dinner or mealtime special as your family sits down together and shares their day.
- Try to keep up with technology and use it to your advantage.
- You may have aches and pains, but don't dwell on them or burden others by complaining. They come with age!"

—

S.C.H.

CHAPTER 2

LEARNING FROM EXPERIENCE, PART 2

Experience is the best teacher.

Latin Proverb

Many well-intentioned people make unwise decisions, experience negative results, and don't understand why. As you can see from reading the previous chapter, I was one of them for years. My intentions were good. I wanted to please God and help people, but I had to realize that working constantly, never taking a day off or a real vacation, and living with barely enough energy to function was not sustainable.

NO ONE IS INVINCIBLE

During the years I worked so hard and stayed so busy, I mistakenly thought that I was invincible, so I kept working harder and harder. I taught and hosted twenty-four to thirty-six conferences each year, and each conference included four or five sessions. Each year, I wrote two or three books, committed to approximately twenty speaking engagements, and did twelve chapel services for our employees. I also did television and radio interviews, along with book signings. Eventually, I added foreign mission trips to my schedule. By that time, I had three teenagers and a toddler.

I look back now and have no idea how I was able to do it all, but I did enjoy the ministry and felt my life was bearing good fruit. God blessed the ministry and gave us favor, and we grew quite quickly. I can truthfully say that all I did was work, and I felt the effects of my schedule more each decade. Then, as I began to reach my senior years, I began feeling its impact differently than ever before. I was less of a visionary, I felt tired physically, and I was weary in my soul. I was also more stressed than ever, and life seemed to be getting more and more difficult.

At the age of sixty-two, I finally began working out with a trainer three days a week and made an effort to eat more healthily. I did start to feel better, so naturally I continued doing what I had always done, which was work. I taught some good messages during that season on entering the rest of God, but I realize now that I did not apply to my own life the truths I taught to others in those messages.

During that season, I also began walking five miles a day and continued doing so for almost three years. The walking gave me energy, but I pushed too hard, not taking any days off. During that time, I had two hip replacements, but during the recovery period I rested only as much as I absolutely had to and went right back to the walking, exercise, and working, working, and working some more!

I wish I'd had a good book on how to take care of myself or had listened to the people who kept telling me I needed to rest, but sadly I didn't. I had to learn by experience. That is usually the most painful way to learn, but it is often the most valuable, because we rarely forget the lessons we learn by going through things.

I FELL APART

I now realize that for years my body tried to warn me that something was going seriously wrong, but I was too busy to pay any attention to the distress signals. One morning in December 2017, I woke up and something had happened in my mouth. It was horribly dry and felt as though it had been scalded. My stomach hurt and I was nauseated. I felt weak and shaky, and my blood pressure was very high. To make a long story short, after seeing three doctors (one of whom said the problem was in my mind and recommended classes on how to control my thoughts) and going to a hospital, where I had every test possible, I received a report. I was told I was very healthy and in good condition for a woman of my age (then seventy-three), but that I had extreme adrenal fatigue. The doctor wrote me a prescription for medication to help with the stress, and I knew I could easily manage taking the medicine each day. But the medicine was not all I needed. The doctor also prescribed resting for at least eigh-teen months! I could do only what I absolutely had to do, he said, *and nothing else*. My family ended up needing to tell me what I absolutely had to do, because I thought I absolutely had to do everything I was doing.

The thought of resting for eighteen months made my mind go blank. I had no idea how to do that! For many of us, rest must be learned; it doesn't come naturally to us. Thank-fully, my family intervened, and we delegated many of my responsibilities to other people. I taught at my conferences, did my television show, and wrote my books. I also did a few other things that only I could do, but mainly I began to learn how to rest and how to let people help me. I have now learned a lot, and I am still learning. I know myself, and while I will always lean toward working, I am definitely attempting to maintain more balance in my life. In fact, I think that right now I have the best schedule I have ever had in my life.

You may feel great and think something such as adrenal fatigue could never happen to you, but I assure you that it could. God created the world in six days and on the seventh day, He rested (Genesis 2:2). God rested! How could some-one who never gets tired need to rest? Perhaps God never gets tired because He does rest. He does not slumber or sleep, according to Psalm 121:4, but I believe He lives in a con-tinual state of rest. God did look at everything He had created and declared it to be good (Genesis 1:31). He took time on that seventh day to enjoy the work He had done on the other six days. We need to follow that example. What is the point in spending our lives working hard at something if we never take time to enjoy the fruit of our labor?

God commanded a Sabbath rest for the people of Israel. Not only did the people receive the instruction to rest, even the land had to rest one out of seven years (Leviticus 25:4). Some people reading this will say, "That is an Old Testament situation. We don't live under those laws because we have a New Covenant under the grace of God."

While we do live under the New Covenant, the principle of needing to rest is just as valid today as it was in Old Testament times. Jesus said, "The Sabbath was made for man, not man for the Sabbath" (Mark 2:27). God gives the Sabbath to us as a gift, and too many people have never opened it. We might say that we owe our bodies one day a week to rest so we can navigate the other six days with vitality and energy.

> God commanded a Sabbath rest for the people of Israel.

By the time I finally realized what I had done to myself at the end of 2017, I owed my body hundreds of Sabbaths. Perhaps you do, too. If we never rest, we spend too much of our energy in the early years of our lives and then have no energy left for the latter years because we have already spent it all. Thankfully, God is a gracious healer. No matter what we have lost, God can help us recover. The psalmist writes, "The righteous will flourish like a palm tree" and "They will still bear fruit in old age, they will stay fresh and green" (Psalm 92:12, 14). I am trusting God for this promise to be a reality in my life, and I hope you will trust Him to do the same in your life, too.

MAKING ADJUSTMENTS

As I write this book, I can look back a couple of years and see that I have made some very positive changes. I am much better than I was, but I know that I have to make permanent changes in my lifestyle. I realize that I am no longer twenty years old—or thirty or forty, or even fifty or sixty. By the time this book is published, I will be seventy-eight, and I have finally admitted it to myself. That doesn't mean that God is finished with me, nor does it mean that I can't work any longer. I still work, but now I work smarter, not harder. I work less than I have ever worked in my entire life, and yet, as a ministry, by the grace of God we are bearing more fruit and reaching more people than ever.

Experience is a great teacher. Even Jesus learned through the things He experienced. According

> *Now I work smarter, not harder.*

to Hebrews 5:8–9, He learned obedience through the things He suffered, and His experience qualified Him to be the Author and Source of our salvation. He was never disobedient, but the experience of being obedient taught Him and equipped Him. If nothing else, my experience has qualified me to bring this message to you and prayerfully, to help you through it.

EVERYONE'S EXPERIENCE IS DIFFERENT

We are all different, and everyone experiences aging differently, but we all do experience changes in our skin, stamina, time needed to recover after events, and other things. I asked a fifty-four-year-old woman who works for us if she had experienced any changes in her body in the past decade. She laughed and then said, "Oh, yes!" She said the main difference she has noticed is that she needs more time to recover from certain activities than she once did. If we pay attention to our bodies, they will help us know how and when to make changes, but if we ignore them, as I did, the result is not good.

Some people have more energy than others. They may have a faster metabolism, or they may be genetically predisposed to high energy. I spoke with our staff pastor, who is in his early sixties, and he said the only difference he sees in himself now compared to his younger years is that his metabolism is slower, and he must be more careful about how much he eats and what he eats in order to maintain his weight at a level he believes is right for him.

I believe that even our personalities play into how we feel. People who are outgoing and laugh a lot quite often feel well. Those who are more laid-back and not bothered by many things often have less stress than those who are uptight. They may also have more energy than others because they do not spend it unnecessarily. Dave is that kind of person. I am an aggressive type-A person who feels the need to solve everyone's problems, and that requires mental and emotional energy. Those of us in ministry have to learn that we are not the saviors of the entire world. Instead, in each situation we face, we would be wise to learn what role we need to play and what we need to do—and then stick to it. That way, we will always have sufficient energy to do what we are called to do. This is my prayer for you, and I have written this book to help you accomplish it.

> *In each situation we face, we would be wise to learn what role we need to play and what we need to do— and then stick to it.*

"I'VE ALREADY HAD MY
ONE-HUNDREDTH BIRTHDAY,
AND ONE THING I HAVE LEARNED
IS THIS: TAKE EACH DAY AS IT
COMES. DON'T WORRY ABOUT
THE FUTURE OR FEEL BAD
ABOUT THE PAST."

—

A.L.S.

CHAPTER 3

HOW TO AGE WITHOUT GETTING OLD

I'm not getting old; I'm getting better.

Author Unknown

There is a story of an elderly woman who understood the power of choice. It illustrates not only the benefits of a positive attitude toward every situation, but also the importance of making good decisions and setting your mind in the right direction.

The lady is ninety-two years old, petite, well poised, and proud. She is fully dressed each morning by eight o'clock, with her hair fashionably coiffed and her makeup perfectly applied, in spite of the fact that she is legally blind. Today she has moved to a nursing home. Her husband of seventy years recently passed away, making this move necessary.

After many hours of waiting patiently in the lobby of the nursing home, she smiles sweetly when told her room was ready. As she maneuvers her walker to the elevator, the staff person provides a visual description of her tiny room, including the eyelet curtains that have been hung on her window. "I love it," she states with the enthusiasm of an eight-year-old having just been presented with a new puppy. "Mrs. Jones, you haven't seen the room...just wait," the staff person says.

Then Mrs. Jones speaks these words: "That does not have anything to do with it," she gently replies. "Happiness is something you decide on ahead of time. Whether I like the room or not does not depend on how the furniture is arranged. It is how I arrange my mind that matters. I have already decided to love it. It is a decision I make every morning when I wake up. I have a choice. I can spend the day in bed recounting the difficulty I have with the parts of my body that no longer work, or I can get out of bed and be thankful for the ones that do work. Each day is a gift, and as long as my eyes open, I will focus on the new day and all of the happy memories I have stored away...just for this time in my life."

The best part of this story is the elderly woman's mindset. She had made up her mind to like her new home before she ever saw it. You and I can have the same mindset toward the aging process. We can see it as an adventure, not something that means we have to be miserable and sit around and do nothing.

I don't know where you are on the aging scale, but you are aging. With each passing day, we are one day older than we were the day before. The time to begin taking good care of yourself and having the right mindset is right now. It is not wise to wait until you're a senior and several parts of your body are in need of repair to begin thinking properly about aging. However, even if you are already a senior, it's never too late to begin.

> *We all need something to do, someone to love, and something to hope for.*

The actor Dick Van Dyke said, "We all need something to do, someone to love, and something to hope for." Anyone can have these blessings. They are not likely to present themselves to people just sitting around wishing for them, but they are certainly available to those who will seek them and go after them.

Having someone to love doesn't necessarily mean having a spouse. We can also love other family members, friends, or acquaintances we volunteer to help. Many people also find having a pet beneficial to them. Everyone needs and wants to be loved, and if we will look for people to love and ask God to send them to us, we will find them.

Dick Van Dyke comes across as ageless despite having danced his way across movie screens since the 1930s. He speaks of having something to do, which I interpret as a sense of purpose—something we must do intentionally, or *on purpose*. Even when people are physically impaired, their purpose can be to pray for and encourage others. There is always someone who needs us, and there is always something we can do to help others.

People who sit home day after day and do nothing but get older amaze me. We can always find ways to be useful if only we will look for them and be willing to try new things.

I believe that age is a number, but getting old is a mindset. How we see ourselves is more important than how many years old we are. Perhaps you have heard the saying "In the end it's not the years in your life that count; it's the life in your years."

I know I am seventy-eight, but I don't sit around and think about how old I am. I think about the life I have lived, and

> *I believe that age is a number, but getting old is a mindset.*

it has been a very good one. I can hardly believe that I am the age I am. I live an active, full life. I work hard at taking care of myself, because I want to last as long as I can. I can't do as much as I once did, and I have less stamina than I once did. The skin on my forearms has gotten thin, and I bruise easily there. I have some arthritis in a few joints. But most of these conditions are normal parts of aging. If you can relate, then remember that these developments don't have to make us feel that we are getting old or that we can't do much. The first time I ever felt that I was getting old was the day I had to sign up for Medicare! I could not believe I was in the Medicare office. The experience felt surreal, as though I were watching a movie about someone else's experience. But I wasn't. It was me, Joyce, in the Medicare office, and I had to realize I simply wasn't as young as I felt in my body or thought in my mind.

I'm glad I don't feel old, and I hope and pray that I never do. I'm dealing with the aging process every day of my life at this point, but I refuse to feel old and think I am finished with life.

While I was writing this book, my daughter-in-law told me about an interesting study she had heard about concerning elderly people. The people conducting the study put several people in their eighties in a nice rest home that was decorated in the style of the 1970s because that was when the people there would have been in the prime of their lives. The result was that they had more energy, more vitality, and more zest for life than they had previously. The way we think about ourselves influences how we respond to aging.

Some people actually talk themselves into not being able to do anything once they reach a certain age. There are other people who look at every milestone as a blessing, some who even view every birthday—not just the "big" ones—as a gift from God. These people enjoy

> *The way we think about ourselves influences how we respond to aging.*

their lives even when they can no longer do everything they once did. They see the adjustments of aging as challenges to be embraced and figured out, not as obstacles to make them stop living.

In 2019, there were approximately 533,000 people on the earth who were more than one hundred years old, and many of them live full and active lives. Not viewing yourself as old won't cause you to avoid all the issues that come with aging, but it will certainly help. Who knows? You or I may live past one hundred years of age. I had a grandfather who lived to be 102 years old, so longevity is in my bloodline.

DON'T COMPARE YOURSELF
WITH OTHER PEOPLE

As the years pass, you may not be able to do all that others your age do, but you can do something, and it is important for all of us to focus on what we can do, not what we cannot do. I cannot lift as much weight at the gym as I did fifteen years ago, but I can still lift a significant amount, and I am doing what I am able to do. Occasionally I say something to my trainer like, "I remember when I could lift a lot more weight when I did bench presses." He is quick to tell me to be glad I can do what I am doing, and always reminds me that I am ahead of the curve. He tells me he has clients that are thirty years younger than I am who cannot do what I do.

> *It is important to focus on what we can do, not what we cannot do.*

This morning at the gym, I had to be reminded of my own message about not comparing ourselves with others. Three other people besides me were in the gym, all in their early twenties. Two were men, so I had no temptation to compare myself to them, but I found myself checking to see how much weight the young woman was using for her various exercises. We had both been using a leg press machine, and I was pressing fifty pounds but noticed she was pressing ninety. I was able to press ninety pounds a few years ago. Without realizing it, I was comparing my seventy-eight-year-old self to a twenty-year-old!

I decided that if she could do ninety pounds, I should at least be able to do seventy pounds, so I increased my weights from fifty to seventy pounds. Later, God helped me realize that I had done exactly what I have been telling you *not* to do—comparing myself with someone else! Human beings have a drive to not simply be as good as others, but be better. This drive often pushes us past our limits and causes us to damage our bodies and our spirits.

Dave has more energy than I do, but we are two different people and have had different things happen to us throughout life. If you are prone to comparing yourself with others, your enemy, the devil, will always make sure someone who can do more than you can is nearby for you to notice. He does not call your attention to all the people who cannot do what you are doing. We are individuals, and God has individual plans for our lives, so we are free to be who we are without trying to be someone we can never be.

Paul writes, "I can do all things through Christ who strengthens me" (Philippians 4:13 NKJV). Nevertheless, we must realize we can do all the things *He* wants us to do, not all the things we want to do.

LETTING GO

I played golf with Dave for twenty years until I started having problems in my wrist and elbow, and now I can't play. I also enjoyed bowling occasionally, and I can't do that anymore, either. While I can't play golf or bowl, I can still write books on my computer and prepare messages to teach at conferences.

I can't wear three-and-a-half-inch spike high heels now, though I wore them until I got bunions and corns on my feet. Then I had to have bunion surgery and have the corns removed. Now I wear comfortable shoes. It's amazing how we persecute ourselves just to be cute! I now prefer comfort over cuteness, unless I can have both.

There are always things we cannot do, especially as we age, but there are also things we can do, and we should focus on those things. We can let the loss of things we were once able to do depress us, or we can decide to be happy with what we can still do.

To say that Dave enjoys golf would be a huge understatement. He *loves* to play golf or even just practice golf. He also enjoys watching golf and reading magazines about golf. I can't think of anything concerning golf that he doesn't like. I asked him how he thought it would affect him as he aged if he ever reached a point where he couldn't play golf, and his answer was, "I've already thought about it and made up my mind to be happy anyway and to find other things to do." Dave's comment represents a healthy mindset toward aging, one that allows us to be happy in any stage of life. If you are already thinking about something you enjoy and telling yourself, "I'm going to be very unhappy when I have to give this up," then you have set yourself up for some sad times. You can avoid those difficult days and find joy in the future instead if you will simply change your mind about the adjustments you will need to make as you age.

> *A healthy mindset toward aging allows us to be happy in any stage of life.*

Focusing on what you do have instead of what you don't have is a wonderful habit to develop. The aging process is a normal part of life, and developing the right mental attitude toward it early in life will be beneficial later. Your latter years can and should be beautiful. One man said, "My wrinkles represent my memories." I like that!

BE CAREFUL HOW YOU TALK ABOUT YOURSELF

Proverbs 18:21 is a powerful verse that teaches us to watch what we say: "The tongue has the power of life and death, and those who love it will eat its fruit." Because words are filled with power and they affect us as well as those who hear them, we should be careful as we talk about aging. Don't repeatedly say, "I'm getting old!" If you do, you will feel old, and others will view you as old. The more comfortable you are with your age, the more comfortable others will be also. The way you view yourself is the way they will view you. If there is something that you can no longer do, instead of saying, "I'm too old to do that," say something like, "Wisdom has required me to stop doing that as I have aged, but I can still do plenty of other things."

> *The more comfortable you are with your age, the more comfortable others will be also.*

Our minds are not exempt from the aging process. For that reason, you may forget a few more things than you once did, but I urge you not to make dramatic statements like "I'm probably getting Alzheimer's" or "I'm getting old and senile." Don't let fear rule your thoughts about yourself and your future. Learn to laugh at yourself when you do silly things, as I do often. Yesterday I broke two dishes at two different times, but I didn't think, *I'm getting old and clumsy.* I thought, *Well, I guess I will clean this up!*

We all experience aging differently. I have noticed that I need more quiet time now than I once did. If too many things are going on around me at one time, I can begin to feel mildly overwhelmed or confused, so I have made adjustments, and I don't feel bad about myself because I need to make them.

> *Learn to laugh at yourself when you do silly things.*

Also, getting eight to nine hours of sleep each night is really important for me. I make sure to do that unless I am doing a conference, in which case I may have a night or two when I only get six or seven hours. At one time in my life, I could write for twelve hours at a time, only getting up to go to the bathroom. Now I need to get up more often, and I can't write more than five hours a day. Many things have changed, but they really have not adversely affected my quality of life.

Life can be just as good or even better than before if we have to let some things go. Everything is for a season, and when the season is over, don't keep holding on to what is no longer beneficial to you.

> *Everything is for a season, and when the season is over, don't keep holding on to what is no longer beneficial to you.*

KEEP MOVING

I appear in front of millions of people on television each day. I don't want them to view me as old and irrelevant, and I purpose not to project that image. Although I am seventy-eight years of age, I don't feel old and I don't act old.

I think some people use their age as an excuse to not do certain things, or to even provoke pity from others, but that is unwise. One of the best pieces of advice I can offer you is to do as much as you can for as long as you can. I have heard that the more we move, the more we can move, and the less we move, the less we can move. Therefore, even when I

> *Do as much as you can for as long as you can.*

am writing, I get up and move around about once every hour. I walk through the house, and then do some mild stretches so my body does not become stiff.

One doctor told me that sitting is considered to be the

new cancer. He meant that sitting for hours at a time is destroying people's health and damaging their bodies. God gave us hundreds of joints throughout our body so we could move, so let's get busy using them. Climb the stairs if you are able to do so instead of always taking the elevator. The walk may do you good! Our natural tendency is to find the easiest way to do everything we do, but perhaps the fact that certain things are easier today than they have ever been is part of our problem.

Some people's greatest need is to move and be more active. Anyone who maintains a sedentary lifestyle is in greater danger of cancer, depression, anxiety, and coronary heart disease, as well as other conditions. The widespread use of computers and social media has caused us to sit more than ever. Although I sincerely appreciate modern technology, we should keep moving and not allow it to make us sit too much. When considering how active we should be, it is wise to use moderation and find a balance. Too much exercise and exertion can be harmful to elderly people, but too little is equally detrimental.

> Anyone who maintains a sedentary lifestyle is in greater danger of cancer, depression, anxiety, and coronary heart disease, as well as other conditions.

I realize that some people have no choice but to be sedentary because of health problems, but many who use a wheelchair can do some upper-body exercises. We should move anything that is movable! When I was recovering from my hip surgeries, I had my trainer come to the house three days a week, and I did upper-body exercises with large rubber bands that are used for exercise. I didn't want to stop moving!

Let me encourage you to get "I can't" out of your thoughts and conversation. Instead of developing the habit of saying, "I can't," try saying, "That would not be wise for me to do at this time in my life." Telling people too often that you can't do this or that anymore because you are old will imprint that impression in your mind and in theirs.

> Instead of saying, "I can't," try saying, "That would not be wise for me to do at this time in my life."

None of us knows for sure how many years we will live, but one thing is for sure: Having a healthy mindset will make all of them worth living.

"LOTS OF PEOPLE WILL COME AND GO OVER THE COURSE OF A LIFETIME, BUT RELATIONSHIPS WITH GOD AND FAMILY REMAIN AND SHOULD BE REPLENISHED, NURTURED, AND CONTINUALLY CULTIVATED."

—

D.F.

CHAPTER 4

SLOWING DOWN THE AGING PROCESS

Self-care is giving the world the best of you, not what's left of you.

Katie Reed

We cannot stop the aging process, because it is part of the cycle of life, but we can slow it down by beginning to take care of ourselves early. For some people, the idea of taking care of themselves seems selfish, but self-care is actually the opposite of selfishness. If we don't take care of ourselves, eventually we won't be able to take care of others, either.

People often make the mistake of thinking they can do without many things that they actually need. They may sacrifice the time they plan to exercise in order to run an errand for a neighbor. Or, even though cleaning house has become quite difficult for them, they may not spend money to get the help they need to accomplish that task because they want to help their adult children buy a car.

While it may be true that people can survive physically without certain things, denying themselves excessively will ultimately decrease their joy and affect them adversely in multiple ways. I frequently hear people say, "I always put myself last," or, "I can do without that. I'd rather give it to someone else." While this attitude can be noble under appropriate circumstances, if it goes too far, it can cause a breakdown in physical, mental, and emotional health. To deny that we have legitimate needs is foolish, and it is not a godly way to live. We all have needs, and if those needs go unmet for too long, the results can be disastrous.

The best gift you can give your family, your friends, and the world around you is a healthy you. If, for example, a mother in a household is always physically drained, mentally overloaded, spiritually dry, and emotionally worn-out, that strain deprives the family of the mother they want and need. She may think she is doing the best thing for her family while she exhausts herself taking care of them and everyone else, but this is a huge mistake and will eventually take its toll on the entire family, including Mom herself.

Learning to say no when appropriate is extremely helpful in preventing premature aging. When I see people in their forties who look older than some people in their seventies, I think it is for one of two reasons: Either they have lived a very hard life, or they have not taken good care of themselves.

Some people's lives are difficult, and they fail to care for themselves properly because they have never learned to say no. They have done too much for too many others and have no energy left to rest, relax, and enjoy life for themselves. Many people who do too much for people find their value and sense of purpose in "doing" for others. Being generous and helpful to others is a wonderful quality, as long as it happens within the context of a balanced life that allows ample time for self-care, too. These people would be wise to recognize when they may be tempted to gain acceptance or feel significant because of what they do for others, and they should ask whether or not what they are doing is God's will for them. If it is not God's will, they need to have the courage to say no.

When people want to hear a yes and get a no instead, they usually are not happy about it, but saying no when you need to may help you live longer and enjoy greater vitality. God never puts more on us than is wise, and even when we are not looking out for our future, He is!

FIVE SIMPLE WAYS TO HELP
SLOW THE AGING PROCESS

When we think about aging, we should remember that every part and function of our bodies ages: teeth, skin, internal organs, bones, hair, eyes, hearing, and everything else. There are some simple things we can do that will help slow down the aging process, but we cannot prevent it entirely. The market is full of anti-aging remedies, and while some may help, nothing stops the clock. I recommend doing all you can do to look and feel as young as possible, but you will get older nonetheless. Aging can be an amazing time in your life if you view the process properly. Here are five simple suggestions.

1. Get seven to eight hours of sleep each night, or more if needed.

You may think there is no way that you can do that, but you can do anything if it is important enough to you. You may have to say no to something else you really want to do in order to get the sleep you need, but adequate sleep and rest will help you age more slowly and feel better as you do.

2. Drink eight eight-ounce glasses of water every day.

Consider this information and you will quickly understand why drinking water is so important:

- The adult human body is up to 60 percent water.
- The brain and the heart are 73 percent water.
- The lungs are approximately 83 percent water.
- The skin is 64 percent water.
- Muscles and kidneys are 79 percent water.
- Even our bones contain water—31 percent, to be exact!

If you live in a dry climate, you need to drink even more than eight glasses of water per day. I occasionally travel to

Park City, Utah, where the altitude is high and the climate is dry, and I almost double my water intake when I am there. The only disadvantage to that is that I spend a lot more time in the bathroom. But if I don't drink a lot of water, my eyes and nose become dry, I develop headaches, and my skin gets very dry. I don't have to drink so much water; the choice is mine, but drinking ample amounts seems to be easier than putting up with the uncomfortable side effects I would have to deal with if I failed to hydrate myself properly.

Clearly, dehydration damages our bodies and prevents them from functioning at maximum levels. I recently met a man who told me that he used to drink at least twelve cups of coffee a day and rarely ever drank water. He is in his early forties and said that he felt well. But after some education on the importance of water, he made a change and started drinking more water and less coffee. He is amazed at how much better he feels. It is entirely possible that people can think they feel all right but have no idea what truly feeling well is like.

Our society offers so many substitutes for water, which makes choosing sugary, chemical-filled drinks instead of healthy, plain water too easy. When people say they don't like water (which is what the man who drank twelve cups of coffee per day told me), the reason is usually that they have not formed the habit of drinking it. If we don't drink enough water, our skin will age more quickly, and many other body functions may operate at a subpar level or even become diseased. My father didn't like water, so he did not drink it, and he died with kidney disease.

3. Get some exercise!

If going to a gym does not appeal to you, then at least get out and do some physical exercise, such as walking or cycling. Weight-bearing exercises help to keep your bones strong. If for some reason you cannot do weight-bearing exercises, there are many other options, including exercising in water, which is easy to move in but still very beneficial to your body, and there are classes that will keep you flexible and balanced while not overstressing your joints or muscles. If you develop the habit of exercising, you will eventually enjoy it and will miss it if for some reason you have to skip it. Our bodies crave what we give them. Give yours what will make it strong and healthy, and that is what it will want.

> *Our bodies crave what we give them. Give yours what will make it strong and healthy, and that is what it will want.*

Dave has been working out with weights regularly for fifty-five years, and he looks amazing. He is eighty-one years old and looks as though he is about sixty-five. His skin is in great shape because the exercise he does sends it oxygen and other nutrients that keep it healthy. Exercise improves circulation, which is good for our skin, cardiovascular system, and other organs.

Remember, we have to keep moving if we want to keep moving. It is easy to think we don't have time to exercise, but once again, we make time for what is important to us. I said for a long time that I didn't have time to exercise, so I have only been doing it regularly for fifteen years. Saying that I didn't have time was simply an excuse not to do it, and I realize that now. I wish I had started much sooner, as I am encouraging you to do, but wishing gets us nothing. Only the proper action at the proper time brings the results we want. Edward Stanley said, "Those who think they have no time for bodily exercise will sooner or later have to find time for illness."

> *We have to keep moving if we want to keep moving.*

4. Take good care of your skin and teeth.

Cleanse your face morning and evening and keep it, as well as the rest of your body, moisturized. As we age, our skin wrinkles and becomes dryer, thinner, and less elastic. Don't spend excessive time in the sun, because that is a sure way to develop skin wrinkles and even dark spots later in life. If you do spend time in the sun, be sure to wear sunblock. I spoke with a skin specialist recently, and she told me that wearing sunblock is one of the most important things we can do to protect our skin. Even sun shining through a car window can damage the skin if we don't protect ourselves from the sun.

Don't go to bed with makeup on. Cleanse and moisturize your face, and let it recover and heal overnight. If you can afford to get professional facials on a regular basis, they are good investments. If you can't, then purchase products you can afford and do the best you can to take care of your skin at home. Coco Chanel said, "Nature gives you the face you have at twenty; it is up to you to merit the face you have at fifty."

Brush your teeth thoroughly at least twice a day and use dental floss, dental brushes, dental picks, or a Waterpik at least once a day to ensure there is no food residue between your teeth. Regular brushing helps prevent cavities and keeps your gums healthy, which helps you keep your teeth. Dental work is expensive and can be uncomfortable, so I encourage you to make caring for your teeth a priority.

5. Eat a healthy diet.

Eat lean meat, plenty of fish, whole grains, and lots of fresh vegetables and fruit. Avoid excessive empty carbohydrates such as breads, crackers, chips, and bakery goods. Limit your sugar and caffeine intake. Don't overeat! Carrying too much weight is ultimately unhealthy in many ways and contributes to fatigue. About two-thirds of Americans are overweight; perhaps that helps explain why so many people are sick.

Take vitamins and supplements on a regular basis. Our food supply today is often depleted of some of the things we need because of the way food is grown or processed. One physician told me that taking vitamins did nothing but give me expensive urine. His opinion was that taking vitamins had no value. However, thousands of other health providers would disagree with him.

I have experienced what happens when we are missing a vitamin or other nutrient that we need, and I have seen how fast we can recover from an unpleasant symptom once that nutrient is restored. Being low on the B vitamins can make us tired. If we are deficient in vitamin B_{12}, it can cause anemia; if potassium is low, it can make us weak and have abnormal heart rhythms. It is interesting to study what each vitamin and nutrient does for your body. Then you can work with your physician to make sure you're getting the vitamins and minerals your body needs.

LAUGH AND HAVE FUN

Laughter has been scientifically proven to improve our health. The Bible states, "A merry heart does good, like medicine" (Proverbs 17:22 NKJV) and "the joy of the Lord is your strength" (Nehemiah 8:10). It is important to laugh and enjoy life, because it helps to keep us healthy and young. I just read that the average four-year-old laughs four hundred times per day, and the average adult only four times per day. I can't guarantee the accuracy of this claim because I see differing opinions in what I read, but without exception everyone says that children laugh much more than adults. We can think, *Of course they do; they have nothing to worry about*, but according to God, we have nothing to worry about either, because He wants to take care of us if we

> *The average four-year-old laughs four hundred times per day, and the average adult only four times per day.*

will trust Him to do so. Learning to cast our care on God is part of learning how to rest internally, and I will cover that later in the book.

When I was in elementary school, our daily schedule included recess each day—a fifteen-minute period of time to play or do whatever we wanted to do. When I went to high school, recess suddenly disappeared without notice and has been missing ever since. Perhaps we would all be better off if we still had a daily recess period. Some states did away with recess for elementary school children, but some of them now realize that children need it and function better with it, so they are reinstating it. It is good for all of us, not just children, to take time to play and have fun.

Some people are simply funnier than others, and I highly recommend having at least two or three friends who have a great sense of humor and can make you laugh. I know someone who once bought a whole book about funny things the queen of England has done and said. This person lives alone and has a job that requires being alone a lot, and sometimes she reads a few pages of the book just to make herself chuckle. I encourage you also to find ways to laugh and make joy a priority.

Some people who look much older than they are have had hard lives and a bad attitude to go with them. They are negative about almost everything and, generally speaking, have a sour and self-pitying attitude. I think it is safe to say that their difficulties in life didn't cause them to age faster, but their attitude did. Some people who face great challenges in life use those challenges to strengthen themselves. They learn from them to enjoy each day no matter what it brings and to keep a positive attitude in all things. Happy people live longer and feel better than unhappy ones.

USE YOUR BRAIN

Keep your brain active by continuing to learn. Read, watch documentaries, take classes, work crossword puzzles, or do whatever you choose to continue keeping your brain curious and engaged in life. In addition, continue to educate yourself on a variety of topics. You are never too old to keep learning. Keeping your brain active will keep you feeling better and slow down mental decline as you age. It also appears to protect the connections among brain cells and perhaps even help you grow new ones. Remember the old saying "Use it or lose it"? Perhaps this maxim applies to our brains as much as it does to other things.

Many people choose to retire at a certain age, which gives them time to do things they enjoy. Some travel, some devote themselves to helping their adult children and grandchildren, some serve in their churches and communities, and some pursue new hobbies.

Though I don't plan to ever officially retire, I do realize that other people do. Retirement allows people to restructure their schedules and gives them time they once spent commuting or working to pursue other interests. This is a wonderful opportunity to keep learning.

I read about a woman who had lived in the same city almost all of her life and had been a

> *Retirement is a wonderful opportunity to keep learning.*

municipal employee for more than forty years. She loved her city very much and knew almost everything important that had happened there over that time, yet she knew very little about its history during the Civil War period through the early 1900s. When she retired, the first thing she did was take a city history class from a local historian. Even though she no longer served her city actively through her job, she found a new way to connect with it and appreciate it. She is one of countless people who turn retirement into a gain instead of a loss. When she finished her class, she knew more than ever about the city she loved.

As I was writing this book, I ran across this story, which also encourages us to keep learning, no matter what our age may be:

The student arrived early, sat front and center, and stood out in my classroom in more ways than one. I'd say that he had about 40 years on his classmates in my undergraduate communications class at California State University, Los Angeles. He eagerly jumped into class discussions, with his self-deprecating humor and wisdom of experience. And he was always respectful of the other students' perspectives, as if each of them were a teacher. Jerry Valencia walked in with a smile—and he left with one too.

"These students gave me the confidence that I didn't need to feel bad about my age," Valencia says.

One day, I spotted Valencia on campus. He said he would have to stop taking classes that semester and reapply for next year. By then, he hoped to have earned enough money from construction jobs and have his student-loan papers in order. But he said he was still coming to campus to attend events or see friends. He asked demurely whether he could still sit in on my communications class.

Sure, I said. But he wouldn't get any credit.

No problem, he said.

Soon there he was again, back at his old desk, front and center, jumping into our discussions on how to find and tell stories in Los Angeles—a 63-year-old Cal State LA junior with as much energy and curiosity as any of the youngsters in class.

For an assignment on changing neighborhoods, Valencia wrote about a favorite local chain restaurant that was "unceremoniously closed." He called it an "earth-shattering" development and a theft of childhood. "It is almost as if someone has stolen that childhood and replaced it with a slippery hill where everything they cherish will slide away," he wrote.

A lot of Valencia's classmates apparently knew he couldn't afford that semester's tuition but was still doing the coursework.

"Here he is, willingly taking a class for the joy of it and benefit of learning," says Jessica Espinosa, a 25-year-old junior. "You don't see that in our generation."

Valencia showed up and took the final exam too. Afterward, students were kibitzing, and I overheard

Valencia say he wanted to stay in school until he earned a master's degree, but it had taken him 12 years to finish community college, so he had a long way to go.

Twelve years?

He was in and out of school, he said, subject to his work schedule and whether he had money for classes. He had earned his associate of arts degree over the summer, then transferred to Cal State LA to start on his bachelor's.

I needed to hear more.

Valencia lives, for the time being, in a mobile home park. He greeted me when I arrived and poured me a cup of coffee.

He told me that his dad had worked at a brick-manufacturing plant and in auto assembly. His mother worked at home. Most of his seven brothers and sisters didn't go to college, and none finished. Valencia is determined to be the first, despite his late start.

He said he was an average student who struggled with math and went to community college a year after graduating from high school but decided quickly it was not for him. He got into construction and then the insurance industry, but he'd always liked to write and do crossword puzzles. "And I loved to read. A lot," he said.

He also loved watching *Jeopardy!* with his mother, and he joked that if one of them ever won the lottery or if he became a *Jeopardy!* contestant, he'd use the winnings for college.

It was around 2007, Valencia said, that he got tired of telling himself he was going to go back. He told his mother it was finally for real.

"When I went back to school, she said, 'I hope you make it, Jerry.' And I told her, 'I'm going to make it, Mom. I'm going to make it.'"

The plan was to capitalize on his construction experience and study civil engineering. But he discovered other interests.

"He was not the youngest student," says Grant Tovmasian, coach of the forensics debate team Valencia joined. "But he was the most motivated and the most dedicated."

Tovmasian says Valencia was a great team player in forensics, encouraging fellow students and inspiring them with his desire to educate himself and live a more fulfilling life.

Valencia's sister Sindi Majors says her brother was always bright, but he went through a couple of rough patches in his life.

"He's pretty much been homeless," says Majors, a retired electrician. She bought him a motor home to help him out, and that's what he lived in from 2009 to 2018.

There is something splendidly irrational about Valencia's determination to get a four-year degree and then a master's. At his current pace, he'll be 90 when he finally hangs all that paper on the wall.

But that doesn't seem especially relevant. He's found all the youthful energy and academic opportunity stimulating.

Valencia's grade in my class this semester will not show up on his transcripts. But I'm giving him an A—and in the most important ways, it counts. (Steve Lopez, "A Man in His 60s Working towards His Masters Proves That You're Never Too Old to Learn," *Reader's Digest*, January 21, 2020; originally published in a slightly different format in the *Los Angeles Times*, December 5, 2018.)

KEEP YOURSELF SHARP

Why do musicians and dancers practice even more than they perform? Practice is what keeps them active and sharp in their skills and talents. If they never practice, their performance will suffer. Likewise, if we don't use our brains unless we absolutely have to, we may find when we really need them that they are not working very well. The same is true physically; if we don't use our muscles, they begin to shrink and atrophy.

> *Feed your mind and body things that will strengthen and nourish them, and they will continue to serve you well even as they age.*

Keep your mind and body active. Feed them things that

will strengthen and nourish them, and they will continue to serve you well even as they age.

MAINTAIN SOCIAL CONNECTIONS

Some people say they prefer to be alone and don't care much for being around other people, but such an attitude is ultimately harmful. We need one another even if we would rather not exert the effort required to make and maintain good relationships. Talking and listening are both good exercises that help us socially. Most people have interesting life stories if we will take the time to listen to them. Listening is one way of showing love to other people.

Our daughter was out shopping one day. As she left a store and walked toward her car, she had to wait by the curb for some cars to pass. An elderly gentleman stood there also, and he began to speak with her. She had several errands to run that day and wanted to leave so she could accomplish them, but she was aware that the man simply needed someone to listen to him for a while. She stood there about fifteen minutes and let him talk. She will probably never see the man again, but listening to him was good for her as well as for him. Giving him her time may have been more important than anything else she did that day.

Do all you can do, as soon as you can do it, to take care of yourself, and it will pay rewards as you age.

"I'VE REALIZED THAT ONE
OF THE SMARTEST THINGS
WE CAN DO AS WE AGE
IS BUILD RELATIONSHIPS WITH
THE WISEST PEOPLE WE CAN
FIND, AND ASK THEM
AS MANY QUESTIONS AS THEY'RE
WILLING TO ANSWER."

—

B.C.

CHAPTER 5

FINDING YOUR NEW NORMAL

When we are no longer able to change a situation, we are challenged to change ourselves.

Viktor Frankl

Normal means usual, and if we do what the people around us usually do, we tend to think we are normal. But I have learned that we all have our own unique type of normal, and as we enter different stages of the aging process, we will often need to find a new normal. Things that were totally normal for us to do during one season of life may be unwise or even impossible at other times.

> *As we enter different stages of the aging process, we will often need to find a new normal.*

When aging or health issues necessitate change in certain aspects of your life, try seeing those adjustments as an adventure rather than as a loss. I recall a time when, due to the growth of the ministry, something that I did not want to change in my life had to change. As I complained about the situation to a wise friend, she said, "You will have to get used to a new normal. What is right for you at this time in your life is your new normal."

Having the proper mindset can make all the difference in how easy or difficult change is for us. Our perspective, or the way we think about things, has the power to help us either enjoy change or resent and resist it. When a change is coming, the first thing we need to do is change our minds about the change. People who refuse to change will never grow.

I remember when Dave and I picked up the ministry mail. On a typical morning, we went to our post office box, retrieved the few pieces of mail that came in, went to a coffee shop, and opened and read it. During those years we did just about everything to keep the ministry going. I answered all the mail on a typewriter. I did all the interviewing and hiring of new employees. Between Dave and me, we made every decision that needed to be made.

> *People who refuse to change will never grow.*

Back then, a normal day for us meant getting up and arriving at the office by 9:00 A.M. and staying there for a full day. That kind of schedule would be abnormal for us now. Not only would it be abnormal, but it would also be wrong for us, because it would prevent us from doing what we need to be doing in this season of our life.

Over the years, especially the past five years, Dave and I have needed to do less and less. We are not as young as we once were, and we need more rest than we did years ago. Now I am at my office three to five days per month. I do most of my work at home, preparing teachings and writing books.

We also travel regularly, but not as much as we once did. For years, we typically did thirty-six conferences per year, plus fifteen to twenty additional speaking engagements. My new normal is twelve conferences a year; writing two to three books per year; doing my television show in the studio at the office; and attending perhaps a total of twelve other events, including board meetings, planning meetings, a chapel service with our employees, and other activities that require our time. But as I have already mentioned, I am amazed that we are now reaching more people, even though we are working less than we've worked at any other stage in our life.

I remember how difficult the decision to do twenty-four conferences a year instead of thirty-six was for us. It meant we had to trust God more, because fewer conferences would generate less income. When we decreased from twenty-four conferences to eighteen, that was also challenging for us, as was reducing the number from eighteen to twelve.

We learned a powerful lesson as we prayed and did our best to use wisdom regarding our conferences, which are big commitments of our time and energy. We learned that following God's guidance concerning the right timing for any changes we make is very important, because where God guides, He will also always provide. Each time we reduced the number of conferences on our schedule, the income we needed still came in, because God is our source, not conferences.

GIVE IT TIME

Anytime we make a major change it feels abnormal at first, but as we give ourselves time to adjust, we grow more accustomed to it. Hopefully we will even begin to like it. I am still getting used to being home more, but it is becoming increasingly normal for me. Now, if I have to be away from home more than usual, I miss being there.

It is amazing how we can dislike something and then end up really liking it. We can hate a change while it is new and later love it so much that we wish we had done it sooner. If something in your life right now is abnormal for you, give it some time, and you may find that you will adapt well to your new normal.

After I got sick in 2017, I was *forced* to make changes. Had I *chosen* to make those adjustments when I should have, I would not have been forced to make them later. I realize now that God was urging me to rest more for a long time, but I was in my flow. Even though that flow was becoming more and more difficult, I didn't see how I could stop.

I mentioned that one of my first disturbing symptoms of adrenal fatigue was a dry, burning mouth. It was so bad at one time that if I talked much, I started to lose my voice. I had to cancel a speaking engagement because of it, and that was very hard for me to do. Because I teach the Bible, I have to be able to speak. Since one of my biggest problems was in my mouth, I was forced to find a new normal.

Problems in the mouth are not the only indicators of adrenal fatigue. I could have had other symptoms, but I might have ignored and pressed through them. But when my mouth was affected, I felt God had me backed into a corner and there was no way out. I *had* to change my way of thinking about how much I could do. I could no longer do it all.

I had to begin to delegate to other people some of my responsibilities and certain things I had always done. That was not easy for me. Watching other people do what I once did was difficult indeed. I had to be careful not to insist that they do everything the way I had done it. By giving them some liberty to express themselves as individuals, many of them not only do what I had been doing, but they do it better than I did it. They are working, I am resting, and the ministry is getting better all the time!

I hope you will learn from my experience. I highly recommend that you change what needs to be changed before you are forced to do so. Life is a series of changes, and to stay healthy and happy, we must embrace the changes instead of fighting them. Despising something that has changed and will never go back to its previous condition is a waste of time. It can make a person bitter and resentful, but it doesn't have to if you choose to embrace it and let it become your new normal.

WHO DECIDES WHAT IS NORMAL?

When Dave wants to do or not do something, he often says, "Well, you know, they say this is best." I always challenge him, asking exactly who "they" are. They are almost always people we do not know! Why would we let of bunch of random people decide what normal is for us? To enjoy the freedom to be our true selves we must push against the magnetic pull of the world and be determined to be unique. Being normal does not mean being like other people in every way. You can be completely normal and still do things in ways that are different from the ways others do them.

The only way to navigate the aging process successfully is to be ready to adapt to a new normal anytime it's necessary. Although this is not a solid scientific fact, it seems to me that aspects of our bodies, minds, and emotions change in some way every decade. For about four decades we are constantly climbing and taking on more and more responsibility. Then, for a couple of decades, things level out and all is well. We know what we are doing, and we can now do it well. It is working, and we may make the mistake of thinking it will never change. But it will. If you have survived multiple decades and are now in the latter part of your life, you probably realize that you are in a season, as I am, when things change more rapidly than they did when you were younger.

> *You can be completely normal and still do things in ways that are different from the ways others do them.*

When we age, our abilities certainly begin to change. But I have found that our desires begin to change also. It is God who gives us the desire and the will to do what pleases Him (Philippians 2:13 NLT). A decrease or the absence of desire is one way that God lets us know a change is coming. When the time came for me to decrease my traveling and speaking, I noticed that I didn't *want* to keep doing those activities as much as I had previously done them. Strangely enough, even though I didn't want to maintain the intensity of my traveling and speaking schedule, I thought I *should* want to maintain it. I wouldn't even admit to people that my desires were changing, because I didn't want them to think I was losing my edge, getting lazy, or giving up on my dreams.

I did not give up on my dreams—I was living my dream! I remember praying with intense tears, begging God to let me help people all over the world. At first I thought I had to be physically present with them in order to do that, but I have now learned I can stay home for a day and reach more people in thirty minutes through television than I could by running all over the world, continually wearing myself out. God has great new ideas and plans for us if we will only be brave enough to let Him give us a new normal.

To take hold of something new, we always have to let go of something old. This is a good thing to do, not a bad thing. When we give up something in obedience to God, He gives us back something better.

I urge you to start letting go and letting God take the lead in your life. Listen to your heart instead of your head, because that is the only way to discern when it is time to make a change.

SETTING BOUNDARIES

The Bible records all kinds of information about boundaries as far back as Old Testament days. It's talking about geographical boundaries, of course, which are simply lines of demarcation to show what land belongs to which people. Those physical boundaries are designed to keep enemies outside of them while keeping citizens safe within them.

Today, we also use the word *boundaries* to describe the limits people set for themselves in relationships or in the ways they will spend their time, energy, or other resources. Those who live without such boundaries live undisciplined, fruitless lives. When we set boundaries in our lives, not everyone likes them or is willing to honor them unless we stand firm in our decision to keep them.

> *Those who live without boundaries live undisciplined, fruitless lives.*

There is no decade in life when we don't need boundaries, though the boundaries may need to be adjusted as each season of life unfolds. In fact, setting some boundaries around your time and energy early in life will help you later. Each of us is responsible for setting and enforcing our own boundaries. For example, if you decide one of your boundaries is that you take one day per week as a "do-nothing day" or a day of rest, stand firm when someone urges you to do something on that day. I can promise you that when you set boundaries, they will be tested. People who don't agree with your boundary will push against it to see if you will take it down. Sometimes these very people need the same boundaries in their own lives, and that is why they cannot respect them in yours. Stand firm, and soon others will accept your boundaries. They may even learn from you to set some boundaries for themselves.

I remember when the phrase "living in the fast lane" was popular and sounded cool to many people. It meant being busy and involved in many pursuits, working hard, playing hard, accomplishing a lot, and probably not sleeping enough while with the "in" crowd. I guess I can say that I lived in the fast lane for about five decades, but I am paying for it in the two or three decades that I have left. If only I had made minor changes years ago, I would not have to make major ones now. But this is my new normal, and I am adapting to it and embracing it.

Do you have safe boundaries in place in your life, or do you just get up each day and try to meet all the demands placed on you without resisting or evaluating what saying yes to certain requests will require of you? Do you try to be available for everybody in your life at all times? Do you say yes when your heart is screaming no?

Maybe the idea of setting boundaries is new to you. Perhaps knowing that setting boundaries around your life is

> *Do you say yes when your heart is screaming no?*

permissible brings you a sense of hope and relief. Many people look at what they do each day and view all of it as simply what they have to do, so they keep doing it until it disables them or even sends them to an early grave. I want to make sure you know this: You have a right to peace; quiet; rest; good sleep; laughter; healthy, high quality-food; and doing some of the things that you want to do. But if you don't insist on maintaining that right, someone will take it away from you by insisting that you need to do something for them.

Based on our individual lives, the demands placed on us vary. Much of the reason I ended up overstressed and unhealthy was because I didn't say no. I should have had better boundaries with at least some of the people who asked me to preach at their friend's church as a favor to them, or to write the foreword for their new book, or to teach at their conference, or to do seemingly hundreds of other things. I still do some of those things, but I do fewer and fewer of them as I age. Those who love me will encourage me to do what I need to do, and they will never be offended if I need to say, "I would love to do it for you, but I just can't at this time in life." When you start setting boundaries, you find out who loves you for who you are instead of what you can do for them.

"Getting older means
dealing with limitations.
The best way to deal with
them is not to resist them,
but to accept them.
Be willing to ask for help
when you need it because
of them. And embrace
them as opportunities
to be creative."
—

M.M.

CHAPTER 6

CAN YOU ALWAYS DO WHAT YOU HAVE ALWAYS DONE?

Only a fool thinks he can always do what he has always done.

Henry Cloud

Henry Cloud's observation about people who think they can always do what they have always done has greatly impacted me. Especially in our younger years, most of us think we will always be able to do whatever we want to do. This is foolish, because the aging process, which is not preventable, demands that we change the things we do. At the very least, aging requires us to change the frequency or intensity of doing them.

I have heard of many people who were known during long seasons of their lives as "an excellent cook" or "a great tennis player." Some have spent long hours in the sun to achieve attractive lawns or fruitful gardens, while others could sew beautifully. These physical activities are important for various reasons. They keep people mentally or physically active, they allow them to set and reach goals, and they provide opportunities for accomplishment and fulfillment. But the longer people live, the more they have to adjust to changing abilities.

No matter how much we enjoy doing certain things right now, it is wise to admit to ourselves that we may not always be able to do them. I think everything changes in some way whether we like it or not. We appreciate being able to say, "This too shall pass," when we are having problems, but this saying also applies when things are going well for us and when we are enjoying our lives.

I do not mean that good things become bad, but that the good in the good things now may eventually have to turn into a different type of good. I firmly believe that what I am doing with my life now is good. I am doing exactly what I should be doing, but it is vastly different from what I used to do, and I know I will need to make additional adjustments in the future.

Youth is a beautiful time in our lives, but our latter years are just as beautiful. We can look at elderly people and think, *They are finished. They cannot relate to the current culture. Their life is basically over. Just look at how wrinkled they are, how white their hair is, and how slowly they walk.* Instead, we should realize that every wrinkle and

> *Youth is a beautiful time in our lives, but our latter years are just as beautiful.*

every gray hair represents an experience, and that all of their experiences would benefit us greatly if we would only respect them enough to stop and listen to what they have to say.

I've often wondered, *If I am no longer able to be in ministry, will anyone ever say to me, "Didn't you used to be Joyce Meyer?"* If they do, it will give me a chance to say, "I'm still Joyce Meyer—just a wiser and more experienced version!" Some people tend to think that when we no longer do what we once did, we are no longer who we once were. That's simply not true. Our value is not in what we do, but in who we are as individuals. Our worth is in our character, our experiences, and whether or not we have truly learned to love God and people.

> *Our value is not in what we do, but in who we are as individuals.*

LEARN TO SEPARATE YOUR "WHO" FROM YOUR "DO"

The most important aspect of your life is not what you do; it is who you become. What value is there in doing all kinds of good deeds but having no love? The Bible says that people who live that way are nothing but a big noise (1 Corinthians 13:1–8). Some people are gifted with a lot of charisma and can impress many others, but they may not have the character required to keep them where their gift has taken them.

How often do we see someone referred to as "a shooting star" or "an overnight success," only to see that person quickly fall and disappear from everyone's memory? This happens far too frequently, and many times it happens because they have talent but no character. They can do or accomplish impressive things, but their character is not developed. When people have talents that will put them in front of a lot of people, it is much better for them to grow slowly and have to work hard to get to the top than to start at the top and then fall to the bottom.

The number of people we could reach through our ministry grew gradually over a period of twenty years or longer. In the late 1970s, I began teaching a Bible study. Twenty-five people attended, and I taught that group for five years. Then I worked at a church for five years and had bigger opportunities there, including teaching a women's group that eventually grew to four hundred, sometimes five hundred, people. Then we branched out and began doing small meetings in hotel ballrooms and banquet centers, where we ministered to seventy-five to a few hundred people. After we went on television, our opportunities grew exponentially. I am still here forty-five years later, doing what God has called me to do.

> *The most important aspect of your life is not what you do; it is who you become.*

Allowing people and organizations to grow slowly is valuable because it gives them time to adjust to the increasing pressures of greater leadership. If people are placed at the top simply because they have an impressive talent and they have not had opportunities to pay the price to get there, the results are rarely positive. During the lean and challenging years I went through in ministry, I learned that who I am as a person is more important than what I do in front of an audience.

The Bible says that we should not put new converts into leadership positions because they will behave stupidly because of pride (1 Timothy 3:6 AMPC). If we are filled with pride, we may mistreat others whom we view as less important than we are. A person who operates this way will have poor moral character and will not set a good example for others to follow. Such people fall quickly, because although others may enjoy their talents, they eventually want to respect those they follow.

There are always exceptions to this point. Some young people may have been taught to develop strong moral character at an early age. Others have had the benefit of excellent parenting and are wise beyond their years. I am not stating that being promoted quickly never works, but more often than not, it doesn't.

YOUR LEGACY

The time will come when you and I will no longer be on this earth. Our lives will hopefully be good memories to others, but we ourselves will be gone. If we believe in Jesus as our Savior and Lord during our earthly lives, then after death we will be living in His presence in heaven. What kind of legacy will we leave behind?

I didn't think much about my legacy when I was young, but now that I am older, I think about it often. I want people to remember me as a godly woman who not only loved God, but loved people as well. I want to be remembered as someone who taught the Word of God accurately in a practical way that helped people live their everyday lives for God. I want to leave a legacy that can still be valuable to people hundreds of years from now if the Lord has not returned by that time.

What is a legacy? It is what we leave behind for others, and I believe the teaching resources and books into which I pour my energy are part of my legacy. Building a legacy that will bless others is one of the biggest reasons I continue to do what I am doing, but I do know that what I do isn't as important as who I am as a person.

> *People may not see us behind closed doors, but God does.*

What we do publicly is often very different than what we do privately, but it should not be that way. People may not see us behind closed doors, but God does. Those with good, tested, and tried character realize that He is always watching what they do. They always try to do their best for Him rather than striving to get other people to admire them.

FINISHING WELL

Near the end of his life, the apostle Paul told Timothy that he had fought the good fight, finished the race, and kept the faith (2 Timothy 4:7). Hebrews 12:1 says that we are to "run with endurance the race God has set before us" (NLT). I want to finish my race well, and I'm sure you do, too.

I believe finishing well means that we are to work with the Holy Spirit to complete the assignment that God has given us. If we want to complete what He has given us to do, we will have to fight against the enemies that try to stop us. We will need to stand strong in faith. We will need to be patient and steadfast, committed and determined. These are all character traits that we develop as we learn to be strong in every season of life.

One of the apostle Paul's most heart-gripping writings is Acts 20:22–24 (AMPC):

> And now, you see, I am going to Jerusalem, bound by the [Holy] Spirit and obligated and compelled by the [convictions of my own] spirit, not knowing what will befall me there—except that the Holy Spirit clearly and emphatically affirms to me in city after city that imprisonment and suffering await me. But none of these things move me; neither do I esteem my life dear to myself, if only I may finish my course with joy and the ministry which I have obtained from [which was entrusted to me by] the Lord Jesus, faithfully to attest to the good news (Gospel) of God's grace (His unmerited favor, spiritual blessing, and mercy).

This scripture has greatly encouraged me to press on many times when I felt like giving up. Finishing what God has given me to do is very important to me, but it doesn't mean that I can always do what I have always done. I will have to adapt and follow God's lead to make changes that will allow me to finish rather than fall apart. I don't believe that anyone can finish their race well if they are not willing to adapt to the changes that are necessary as they age.

We should embrace where we are in each stage of life and enjoy our journey toward the finish line. Don't be one of those people who always talks about the "good old days." Those days are over, and they will never be repeated, but new and even better days are ahead if we will embrace them.

"As I've grown older, my capacity for handling stress has diminished. To deal with stress better, I try to:

- Fight fear of the unknown with God's help and His Word.
- Assure myself that slowing down isn't bad; it's a healthy thing to do as I age.
- Ask for help when I need it, and let go of pride that prevents me from asking for it.
- Not hang on to negative emotions, but remain positive with God's help.
- Go for walks and stretch or exercise regularly.
- Focus on what's important. Let go of nonessential things.
- Memorize Scripture and recite it when stressed or going to sleep.
- Make every day count."

—

C.E.

CHAPTER 7

A HEALTHY UNDERSTANDING OF STRESS

Calmness is the cradle of power.

J. G. Holland

One reason I rejected the diagnosis of stress over the years was that I thought it meant that I was weak and couldn't handle life. My mother suffered from many stress-related issues, and after watching her go through a nervous breakdown, I was determined not to have the same problems she had. She was never a strong person emotionally, and she had very little confidence. Her weakness kept her from confronting my father about sexually abusing me, and although I didn't hate her, I did grow up hating weakness. I viewed being sick due to stress as a weakness, so I rejected it.

Everyone encounters stress. God has equipped the human body to handle a reasonable amount of stress, but being under excessive amounts of stress for a long time does damage in a variety of ways. For years, I had severe headaches. One time I was ministering at a church in Florida and mentioned to the pastor that I had a horrible headache. He suggested that I allow a massage therapist who attended the church to massage my neck and shoulders. I had never had a massage, and I really didn't think it would help me, but I agreed to try it.

When she began massaging the back of my neck, especially at the very base of my skull, the pain was so intense I could barely stand to let her continue. She said the tightness resulted from a buildup of stress that kept me from being able to relax my neck muscles. She worked on me for about thirty minutes, and when she stopped, my headache was gone. Since that time, I've gotten massages whenever possible, because they are so effective at relieving stress stored in our muscles.

Stress is part of life. No one can completely avoid it, but we can learn to manage it. If we pay attention to our bodies, we can learn what signals they send to let us know when the stress is becoming too much. These indicators include feeling tense, being unable to relax, and experiencing physical pain somewhere. When we work out, we place stress on our bodies, but this is actually good stress that relieves the wrong kind of stress. We are working the muscles that store stress, getting oxygen to them, and causing them to release tension. This ultimately makes us feel better and more relaxed.

One reason exercise helps us so much in the aging

process is that although we have stress, we release it regularly through regular exercise. This way, it doesn't have an opportunity to build to the point that it damages our bodies and emotions.

Google's online dictionary defines *stress* as "pressure or tension exerted on a material object; a state of mental or emotional strain or tension resulting from adverse or very demanding circumstances." Since we cannot always avoid adverse and demanding circumstances, we need to do things that will release the stress while we are in the midst of them.

Some people face more adversity than others. They may live with financial pressure, marital strain, or chronic sickness. They may have a special needs child who requires extra care and attention or have responsibilities to care for aging parents. Realizing the stress you are under and making an effort to do something to relieve it is one way to take good care of yourself. To do so, consider:

- Resting or taking a nap when you need to rest
- Doing something fun
- Laughing
- Getting a massage
- Treating yourself to a facial
- Devoting time to a hobby you enjoy
- Sleeping seven to eight hours each night
- Taking a leisurely walk
- Taking a hot bath
- Breathing deeply

I have also found that taking what I call a five-minute vacation is very helpful to me. My usual pattern is to go from one thing to another until everything is done, but now I stop between activities, especially if I feel even slightly tired. I sit in my recliner for just five minutes to relax and breathe.

When we feel stressed, we generally hold our breath, or we don't take as many breaths per minute as normal. Normal breathing is twelve to twenty breaths per minute, but I often find myself holding my breath when I am stressed. Simply relaxing and breathing regularly helps me. I have even experienced a headache going away simply because I stopped and made sure to breathe deeply and properly.

LACK OF KNOWLEDGE

God's Word teaches us that people perish for a lack of knowledge (Hosea 4:6). This has certainly proven true for me in regard to my health. Through all the years I built up stress that ultimately climaxed in severe adrenal fatigue, I had no idea what I was doing to myself. I wish I had been able to read a book like this one forty-five years ago, because it might have helped me avoid some of the problems I have had to deal with.

For example, I have heard that airplane travel is very hard on our bodies. I have traveled by air regularly for more than forty years, but I had no idea it was so stressful. When I was tired the day after flying, I always thought, *I shouldn't be tired! All I did was sit on a plane.* Now I know that flying is stressful.

Let me encourage you to give yourself permission to be tired. You don't need a reason or an excuse. If you are tired, rest! If you feel you are excessively tired, see your doctor. But if you are tired simply because you are aging, accept it as a new normal and take a break or a nap.

We learn things all the time, but they are not always the things we need to know. Some lessons children learn in school don't help them prac-tically, while others could be invaluable to them later in life. For example, think about the

> *Give yourself permission to be tired.*

huge number of people who have back problems. What if we were taught early in life how to properly take care of our backs? What if we learned as young people the right and wrong ways to pick up heavy items? For years, I used my back when picking up objects, and I didn't find out until I was sixty years old and having back problems that we should use our leg muscles to squat and pick up things instead of bending and using our backs. Even teaching young children to maintain good posture could help them avoid back prob-lems later in life.

I recommend that while you are young you study how to maintain good health in every area of your body. You may feel so well and strong now that you think it would be a waste of your time, but just the opposite is true. It could be the key to continuing to feel well for years to come.

We can learn from experience what places the most stress on us. We are all different, and what one person can do with ease may be really difficult for someone else. I know, for example, that hurrying puts a lot of stress on me. I have also learned that when too many things are coming at me at once, it puts me on what I call overload. I used to brag frequently about being a great multitasker, but I definitely have noticed that since I have gotten a bit older, I need to take things one at a time.

The changes I finally made took time to make *and time to accept*. I had to learn that the fact that I can no longer do things the way I once did does not mean I am old and incapable. It simply means I need to change and adapt. Stopping something you should no longer be doing is just as important as starting things you should be doing. However, if you have the desire to keep doing it, I suggest looking for ways to adapt or remain involved in it instead of giving up on it quickly.

> *Stopping something you should no longer be doing is just as important as starting things you should be doing.*

THE STRESS VIRUS

Excessive stress has become like a virus afflicting almost everyone. For many people, living under intense pressure is their new normal. Just think, for example, about social media and the many interruptions it brings into our lives daily. The dings and beeps of electronic devices have started to control us. I often have my phone in my purse, and I am amazed how many times it beeps, no matter what I am doing. When I hear it, I feel the need to find out who wants me and what they have to say. While technology has given us quick access to almost anyone and anything, and it definitely has its good qualities, it has also added a lot of stress to most people's lives.

We really shouldn't blame social media and our cell phones for the stress we experience because we are available almost all the time. Managing our availability is our responsibility. Cell phones and devices don't control us; we control them. We must manage them in ways that help us, not in ways that add stress to our lives. Becoming accustomed to instant availability has made us more impatient than ever. I strongly urge you to *enjoy modern technology as long as it is truly adding to your life and not stealing it or causing you unnecessary stress.*

Dave answers emails when he feels like responding to them, so if you email him, you might not get an answer for two weeks. He handles text messages and even answering his phone the same way. All of these methods of communication offer him benefits, but he does not let them control him. Sometimes his way of dealing with them annoys me if I am the one trying to contact him, but I have seen that managing communications as he does keeps him peaceful and not stressed.

I remember when, if people were in the car and wanted to make a phone call, they had to find a public pay phone, park the car, get out, and hope they had correct change in order to make the call. I also still remember having a four-way party line on our home phone. Four families shared the same phone line, so having to wait quite a while to gain access to an available line was common. Today we feel stressed if we are driving in an area that does not have adequate cell service and we have to wait just a few minutes until we reach a different service area. Most of us can remember not very long ago when we could not have imagined being stressed over something like that!

Some people seem to feel abnormal if they don't feel rushed and stressed. I think it is possible for people to become addicted to constant activity and reach the point where they cannot slow down even when they want to.

Let me encourage you: Instead of saying repeatedly to anyone who will listen, "I am so stressed I can hardly stand it," start doing something about it. You may need to learn the lesson I learned years ago, which was that I was the one who filled my calendar with commitments and responsibilities, so I was the only person who could change it. Understanding this can change your life in a wonderful way, so I'll repeat it: You make your schedule, and you are the only person who can change it. True, not everyone will be happy if you don't make yourself instantly available, but it will help you live longer and age more slowly.

> *You make your schedule, and you are the only person who can change it.*

Stress is making people sick and even shortening the life span of some. It also has a negative impact on our quality of life. The older we get, the less stress we can manage well. This is one reason we should really pay attention to our bodies and God's voice speaking to our hearts and make changes when they urge us to do so.

The life you have is your life. It is a gift from God, and you are wise not to allow other people's demands to steal it from you.

"An increasing intimacy
with the Lord will grace
your life as you age
like nothing else will.
Keep allowing Him
to continue to do
'a good work in you,'
as Philippians 1:6 says,
all the days of your life."

—

M.E.F.

CHAPTER 8

STAYING STRONG SPIRITUALLY

Be strong in the Lord and in his mighty power.

Ephesians 6:10

I wouldn't say I've had an easy life, and you may feel the same way about your life. My life has been amazingly good, but it has also been hard. I read about a woman who had suffered greatly, yet said, "I've had a good hard life." I'm sure you know what she means. You keep going, and you don't intend to give up, but you sure wish life would get easier at times. One thing that can sustain us through any kind of trouble is staying strong spiritually.

The strong spirit of a man sustains him in bodily pain or trouble, but a weak and broken spirit who can raise up or bear?

Proverbs 18:14 AMPC

This scripture has sustained me through many hard times. When we cannot make a problem go away, we can still stay close to the Lord and remain strong in Him because His strength will sustain us even when our strength is all spent. God tells us in His Word that rest and quiet bring strength.

> This is what the Sovereign Lord, the Holy One of Israel, says: "In repentance and rest is your salvation, in quietness and trust is your strength."
>
> Isaiah 30:15

Life holds many situations that we cannot change, but when we reach the point where we don't think we can bear the pressure, we are not out of options. God is always with us and always ready to help if we will seek Him.

Each of us is a spirit being, we have a soul, and we live in a body. Each part of us needs to be strong at all times. Just as our bodies need food regularly in order to be strong and function properly, so do our spirits.

FEEDING THE SPIRIT

The spiritual part of our nature feeds on God's presence and His Word. Both are accessible all the time, but we have to choose to partake of them. God is never more than one thought away, and merely turning our thoughts to Him and away from our troubles can give us the strength to press on.

I have identified forty benefits that the Word of God

provides for us. I am including the list, titled "Forty Things the Word of God Does for You," for your convenience, but if you want to recommend it to anyone else, it can be found online at joycemeyer.org/study in the "Ready for More?" section at the bottom of the page.

1. The Word of God is truth, and when we follow it, we are made free (John 8:32).
2. The Word is life, healing, and health to all who find them (Proverbs 4:20–22).
3. The Word heals and delivers us (Psalm 107:20).
4. The Word protects us (Psalm 18:30).
5. Meditating on the Word brings wisdom, prosperity, and success (Joshua 1:8).
6. The Word brings stability, fruitfulness, and fulfillment, and all that we do will prosper (Psalm 1:3).
7. God's Word upholds, guides, maintains, and propels the universe (Hebrews 1:3).
8. God's Word has the power to create (Genesis 1).
9. Those who order their conduct and conversation according to the Word are blessed (Psalm 119:2).
10. The Word cleanses and purifies us (Psalm 119:9; John 15:3; John 17:17; Ephesians 5:26).
11. The Word reduces the capacity to sin. It strengthens us against temptation (Psalm 119:11).
12. The Word revives and stimulates us (Psalm 119:25; Psalm 119:50).
13. God's Word enables us to walk at liberty and at ease (Psalm 119:45).

14. God's Word is filled with promises to give us mercy and grace (Psalm 119:58).

15. God's Word gives us good judgment, wise and right discernment, and knowledge (Psalm 119:66).

16. God's Word is better than thousands of gold and silver pieces (Psalm 119:72).

17. God's Word makes me wiser than my enemies (Psalm 119:98).

18. The Word is a lamp to our feet and a light to our path (Psalm 119:105).

19. When we are afflicted, God's Word quickens us and gives us life (Psalm 119:107).

20. God's Word gives us hope (Psalm 119:114).

21. The entrance of God's Word brings light and dispels darkness (Psalm 119:130).

22. God's Word brings direction and shows us what to do (Psalm 119:133).

23. Jesus is the Word (John 1:1; John 1:14; Revelation 19:13).

24. The Word of God, when planted and rooted in our hearts, has the power to save our souls (James 1:21).

25. God's Word strengthens us (Psalm 119:28).

26. God's Word melts hardness in our hearts (Psalm 147:18).

27. The Word often brings persecution (Mark 4:17).

28. The Word transforms (changes) us into God's image (2 Corinthians 3:18).

29. God's Word is a weapon against the devil and armor that protects us in warfare (Ephesians 6:17).

30. God's Word renews our mind (Romans 12:2).
31. God's Word destroys mental strongholds (lies) and teaches us the truth (2 Corinthians 10:4–5).
32. The Word divides soul and spirit (Hebrews 4:12).
33. God's Word comforts and consoles us (Psalm 119:50).
34. The Word helps us see the error of our ways and turn in God's direction (Psalm 119:59).
35. God's Word causes us to delight even in the midst of trouble and anguish (Psalm 94:19).
36. The Word gives us great peace (Psalm 119:165).
37. God's Word abiding in our hearts makes us victorious over the wicked one (1 John 2:14).
38. We are born again (regenerated) by the ever living and lasting Word of God (1 Peter 1:23).
39. The Word of God endures forever, and it is good news (1 Peter 1:25; Mark 13:31).
40. God's Word contains self-fulfilling power (Isaiah 61:11).

You can see as you read through this list that God's Word is extremely valuable and certainly worth an investment of your time to study and meditate on it. You will be amazed at how strong and encouraged God's Word will keep you through every season of your life.

Probably what has plagued me the most throughout the years is a variety of physical problems—from headaches to hurting feet and everything in between. The ailments were never enough to stop me, but they did make life more difficult, and they did require me to need more faith and spiritual strength to keep going. Whether it was a bunion on my foot, plantar fasciitis in my heel, pain in my wrist due to a tear in a tendon, breast cancer, or a back injury, it seemed I experienced a stream of little nagging conditions. As I prayed and practiced patience, God healed me or provided answers for each situation, and then soon some other little nagging thing would come along. Each one took my time to deal with or tried to distract me and keep my focus off of my purpose.

At this time in my life, I am dealing with a shoulder that hurts. After a doctor's appointment, an X-ray, and an MRI, I was diagnosed with calcium deposits on my rotator cuff. Now I need to get a cortisone shot to see if that helps. God never promised us we would not have trouble in this life, but He did promise to always be with us and to help us. We should take care of everything we can take care of and trust God to take care of everything we cannot take care of, while doing our best to stay focused on our assignment from Him in the meantime.

Perhaps you relate to my story. Your nagging problems may not be health related. They may be in the area of finances, relationships, fear, or something else. But having problems doesn't mean that you don't have victory. If you love God, serve Him, help people, and have a good attitude in the midst of difficulty, I think that is a greater victory than having no problems.

> *Having problems doesn't mean that you don't have victory.*

Jesus faced challenges and difficulties while He was on

earth, as did the apostles and multitudes of others, but they all found strength in God to help them press on and do His will.

The apostle Paul wrote that a "wide door of opportunity" opened to him and with it came "many adversaries" (1 Corinthians 16:9 AMPC). He also said that when he tried to do good, evil always came (Romans 7:21). These verses teach us that our challenges should not surprise us, but neither should they intimidate us. We are more than conquerors through Jesus Christ, who loves us (Romans 8:37).

In his letter to the Corinthians, Paul writes that in order to keep him from becoming conceited, he was given a thorn in the flesh, a messenger of Satan to torment him. Three times he prayed and asked the Lord to remove it, but God said, "My grace is sufficient for you, for my power is made perfect in weakness" (2 Corinthians 12:7–9).

Many theologians and Bible scholars have discussed and disagreed about what Paul's thorn was. To me, the point is that it was from Satan and it tormented him. He asked God to take it away, and God chose not to do so. Instead God told him that He would give him enabling grace to live with the thorn in the flesh and do what he was called to do. This kept Paul humble and leaning on God.

You may not agree with this, but I think that sometimes the greater the degree to which God uses us, the more of these little thorns we may experience. Why? They force us to lean on God and to constantly remember that apart from Him we can do nothing (John 15:5). If we never have problems, how can we have compassion for those who do? Paul writes that

God comforts us so that we can comfort others with the same comfort we have received from Him (2 Corinthians 1:4).

Satan always tries to stop anything good and anything that will help people. We need spiritual tenacity to keep going in the face of opposition, and this will only be possible if we take time to stay spiritually strong.

> *If we never have problems, how can we have compassion for those who do?*

Some people think they are too busy to spend time in prayer and Bible study, but not making time for these investments in our spiritual lives is one of the biggest mistakes we can make. Prayer is simply talking with God, pouring out our hearts to Him, letting Him know that we need Him and can't do what is before us without Him. Bible study is reading and studying God's Word. His Word has power inherent in it; it feeds us and makes us strong. Even if we are reading verses or passages we have read hundreds of times before, reading them again is still beneficial. Think about it: We eat the same foods over and over again because we like them. Reading and studying God's Word should be no different.

If I need peace, I know several scriptures I can read that will calm me down. If I need healing, I know several verses to go to and find promises that God will heal me. If I need finances, I know many scriptures that will assure me that God will provide for my every need. I don't think we can have a problem for which God's Word does not have the answer. His Word encourages us, strengthens us, heals us, corrects us, enlightens us, and provides us with many other blessings.

I recently wrote a book on Proverbs, called *In Search of Wisdom*, and one thing that impressed me about Proverbs is how many principles are repeated again and again in this one book of the Bible. This convinced me completely that God believes we need repetition in order to stay strong in any area of our lives. For example, I found in just one chapter perhaps seven scriptures on the words of our mouth, and then six more in the next chapter. At times, the Holy Spirit led the writer to teach the exact same principle in several chapters. I urge you to never tire of reading and studying the same truths and lessons over and over in Scripture, because they feed you each time you do.

Never approach prayer or studying God's Word as an obligation to be fulfilled; approach it as a privilege to be enjoyed. The Word of God is medicine for our souls, and we should take our medicine regularly, just as a person who needs physical healing should do. God's medicine—His Word—has unlimited refills, and its side effects are life, healing, strength, joy, and restoration.

STRENGTH FOR AGING

Aging can be challenging, because it involves changes in our bodies, our strength, and our abilities. But we never need fear that life will become too much for us, because God will always give us all the strength we need. If we need more strength from Him as we age, we can fully expect to receive it. However, we do need to be obedient to make any changes that He leads us to make in our lifestyle.

> God is our refuge and strength, an ever-present help in trouble.
>
> Psalm 46:1

The Lord won't strengthen us to do things that are not in His will for us, but He will always strengthen us to do

> *The Lord won't strengthen us to do things that are not in His will for us.*

what He wants us to do. I like to say that God gives us "grace for our place." Wherever God has you and whatever your circumstances are, He will give you grace—favor, power, ability—to do what He has for you to do.

Do you ever look at someone else's life and think, *They experienced so much difficulty, and I wonder how they did it?* I heard of a woman who lost all of her children at one time in a house fire, and I remember saying those very words. God gives us grace to endure what He allows in our lives and to not be bitter if we will receive it from Him. Another word I like for *grace* is *ease*. Grace makes difficult and even impossible things much easier than they would be without it.

You will need more supernatural strength as you age, but thankfully you should also have more time to seek God and study His Word so you can receive it.

"If I could sit down today with a young person and share some wisdom about aging, I would talk about staying close to the Lord and being led by the Spirit. I would also talk about the importance of rest and the benefits of strength training. Both of these have physical and mental benefits. We have a biblical responsibility to stay strong in body, mind, and spirit."

—

F.D.

CHAPTER 9

AGING GRACEFULLY

Life is 10 percent what happens to me and 90 percent how I react to it.

John Maxwell

When I say that I want to age gracefully, I mean that I want to grow older with a good attitude, and I don't want to make the process difficult by resisting every change that needs to take place. I don't want to feel sorry for myself because I can't do everything I once did or because I don't look the way I once did. I want to be thankful for all that God has done for me, all He has safely brought me through, all He has allowed me to do, and all He still allows me to do.

I think grace and gratitude go together. The more grateful I am for the grace I currently have, the more grace I will get in the future. We hear the word *grace* often in the Christian community, but perhaps we don't appreciate grace as we should because we don't fully understand it.

We are saved by grace through faith in Jesus, not because of any works we have done (Ephesians 2:8–9). Grace is said to be "God's riches at Christ's expense," or the undeserved favor of God; it is that, but even more. Grace is also the power and anointing (enablement) of the Holy Spirit for us to do what we need to do in life. Grace is the power that changes us into the image of Christ as we grow spiritually. We cannot change

> *The more grateful I am for the grace I currently have, the more grace I will get in the future.*

ourselves, nor can we add more of God's favor to our lives through effort or by trying to be good or perfect. We receive God's grace by faith. It was extremely helpful to me when I learned that grace is God's power coming to us freely through our faith, making what would be hard or impossible for us something we can do with ease.

We certainly should desire to do good things to glorify God, but we do them by His grace, not self-determination. We do need to be determined, but even that is a gift of God's grace. There is grace and more grace available (James 4:6); we receive the grace we need by releasing our faith and trusting God to do through us what we cannot do without Him. We are partners with God. He gives us ability, and through Him, we do what He leads us to do. He won't do our part, and we can't do His part.

BE GRACIOUS

We can learn to age gracefully by enjoying our journeys through life and living graciously with a good attitude. We can stay sweet and kind instead of becoming cranky and crabby because life is not what it once was.

Gracious people are kind and tactful, and they never attempt to hurt others with their words or actions. They treat others with respect. Possibly more than anything else, a gracious person is thankful and says so.

As we age, our bodies may not feel quite as good as they once did. They may even feel quite a bit worse than they once did, depending on how well we have taken care of ourselves over the years, our genetics, and other factors. A friend of mine has a ninety-five-year-old aunt who has never taken medicine or been hospitalized. She has smoked all of her life and has never eaten a healthy diet. She has done everything health experts say *not* to do, yet she still lives alone and manages her life by herself. One thing she has done right is that she has always had a great attitude and is happy.

> Whether we feel great or not so great, it is important to remain kind, uncomplaining, and thankful for what we have.

I am certainly not suggesting we can make all the wrong choices concerning our health and have everything turn out all right as long as we have a good attitude, but I share this story to show how powerful a positive attitude can be. I think it is safe to say that people who have consistently positive, happy attitudes will have fewer health problems and most likely live longer than those who are negative and sour.

Whether we feel great or not so great, it is important to remain kind, uncomplaining, and thankful for what we have.

We should not be mean-spirited toward others because we don't feel well or because we are going through changes that we don't like. As we age, we may need help from others. If so, it is important to always be kind and show appreciation for what they do for us.

My children do a lot for me that makes my life easier and frees me to be able to keep teaching God's Word and writing my books. I tell them very frequently how much I appreciate them.

> *Needing help is not a sign of weakness!*

When you get to the point where you need help, don't let pride prevent you from asking for it. Needing help is not a sign of weakness!

OUR ODDITIES

I started praying years ago that as I got older, I would stay sweet and be funny. My children and Dave all tell me I am very funny, but it is actually the things we do as we age that are funny.

I sometimes look for my phone while I'm talking on it or look for my glasses while they are on my face. Sometimes I tell my children they didn't tell me something, and they insist they have told me twice before. When these conversations first began to take place, I argued that they had not told me, but now I simply assume they are right, because they probably are.

Dave can't hear as well as I can, but his eyesight is better than mine because he had Lasik surgery and I am not a candidate for it. When we watch television, he says, "What did they say?" or, "Turn up the sound," several times throughout a show or movie, and I can't read anything about the movie unless the print is large or I am wearing my glasses. Dave said the other day, "We can help each other, because I can tell you what the movie is about, and you can tell me what they are saying." I recently asked him what he thinks we will be like in another ten years and he said, "I'll probably say 'huh' four times instead of twice when you're talking to me." We have fun together and tease each other about our uniqueness.

Part of aging gracefully is not taking yourself too seriously, because you will probably do some things that are very funny and not even realize you are doing them. You may put things away and not remember where you put them. You may try to wash your face with sunblock, as I did recently. Instead of thinking that you are falling

> *Part of aging gracefully is not taking yourself too seriously.*

apart or, even worse, that you are stupid, just have fun with situations such as these.

It is impossible for any of us to be the same at seventy or eighty years of age as we were at thirty or forty. Growing older—and all that goes with it—is part of the cycle of life, and it can be beautiful if we walk through it graciously and have the right attitude toward it. You can start preparing yourself now for your latter years by planning to have a good attitude, expecting them to be a wonderful time in your life, and looking forward to what God has for you in that season.

I now need more grace to get up in the morning than I used to, and I need more grace to stay out late at night when needed. I understand the importance of asking for and receiving God's power to help me do things that I once did very easily, so I ask for it frequently. My family teases me because when I go out during the day, I like to be home by late afternoon whenever possible. I'm sure they will begin to feel the same way as they age. When you have spent fifty or sixty years being out doing something every night, you will probably want to stay home too. There really is no place like home!

Dave and I also like to eat our main meal of the day by 3:00 P.M. if possible. I don't like going to bed on a full stomach, and I go to bed early. I prefer to go to sleep about 9:00 P.M. and get up between 5:00 and 6:00 A.M.

As you age, you will find that you become more particular about how you do things. You create a routine that works for you, and you won't like to be out of your routine for too long. We usually refer to this as being "set in your ways." I don't feel bad because I am set in my ways concerning being at home. I don't like to stay out at night. I've earned the right to stay home if I want to. By the time you have lived several decades, you too have earned the right to your own brand of being particular.

When I think about aging gracefully, one thing that catches my attention is that although I have seen decline in

> *As you age, you will find that you become more particular about how you do things.*

some of my abilities, when it comes to teaching God's Word or writing, I am just as sharp as I ever was. This is because God is giving me extra grace to keep doing what He wants me to do, and you can trust Him to do the same for you. If He ever stops giving me the grace to do it, that will mean He doesn't want me to do it anymore. We can only do what God enables us to do and should not try to force ourselves into something that simply isn't working. We should do what God guides us to do with all of our hearts, and when He wants us to lay it down and do something else, we should do it graciously.

"I KNOW A FEW PEOPLE WHO HAVE FOLLOWED GOD CLOSELY AS THEY HAVE AGED. AT EACH INTERSECTION OF LIFE, THEY HAVE MADE THE ADJUSTMENTS HE HAS LED THEM TO MAKE. IN EVERY SEASON, THEY'VE REMAINED COMMITTED TO CONTINUAL MATURITY AND CONSISTENT SPIRITUAL GROWTH, EVEN AS THEIR PHYSICAL ACTIVITIES AND ENERGY LEVELS DECREASED. THEY ARE GREAT EXAMPLES!"

—

E.A.M.

CHAPTER 10

DISCERNING GOD'S WILL

Do not be foolish, but understand what the Lord's will is.

Ephesians 5:17

Knowing God's will for their life seems to be challenging for many people. However, it isn't that difficult if you understand how to discern the flow of God's grace in your life. Discernment functions in the spirit rather than the soul, and it is a very important spiritual ability to have. Let me use a personal example to help explain how discernment operates. My mind and emotions may urge me to take a certain action or make a certain decision, but if I have no peace about it, that usually means my spirit is discerning that it is not right for me, even though I may not understand why. In such instances, we choose to trust God, knowing that He always leads us in what is best, even if we do not understand the reasons for it.

Desire is involved in finding and following God's will. I don't believe that God calls us to spend most of our lives doing things we are not interested in and have no desire to do. Multitudes of people work at jobs that they hate for most of their lives because they never have the courage to step out in faith and follow their heart's desire. Perhaps they make a lot of money doing work they don't enjoy, and they choose finances over being fulfilled and content by being in God's will. Let me ask you: Are you doing what makes you happy? Do you love your job? I love my job, and I believe that if you are doing what God wants you to do, you will love yours, also.

> *I don't believe that God calls us to spend most of our lives doing things we are not interested in and have no desire to do.*

There are some jobs that may not be totally pleasant every minute of every day, but for some reason you sense a purpose in them and feel you need to do them for a season. You may not be out of God's will doing what you are doing now, and work itself is honorable. God permits many things that are not His perfect will. He also uses everything you do to educate you and give you experience or relationships that will be valuable when you finally move into that for which He has created you.

If you are doing something that is not God's will, there will always be struggle and frustration, and it will be hard and unfulfilling. You will not feel a sense of purpose, but will feel you are simply passing your time so you can get paid. If we are in God's will, there will be an ease to what we do. We will desire to do it and experience open doors (opportunities) and provision.

I did a variety of jobs before becoming a Bible teacher and an author. They were not bad; they just were not the thing for which God had designed me. I didn't hate those jobs, but neither did I love them like I love teaching God's Word.

In the Book of Acts, while the believers in the early church were worshipping the Lord and fasting, the Holy Spirit said, "Set apart for me Barnabas and Saul for *the work to which I have called them*" (Acts 13:2, emphasis mine). Barnabas and Saul (who was also called Paul) had been active in ministry for several years, but here we find the Holy Spirit saying there was something specific He wanted them to do. What you do may change as you travel through life, but when you find the thing God has called you to, it will affect you differently than anything you have ever done before. We may do many good things in life, but they may not be the best God has for us. The fact that we *can* do something doesn't necessarily mean we *should* do it.

Let me encourage you to search your heart and ask yourself if you truly believe you are doing what God desires you to do or merely doing something to bring home a paycheck. Perhaps you work in an office as a secretary, but the real desire of your heart is to be a nurse. Or you may work in a factory, but your true desire is to own your own small business.

I know God has something for you to do that you will enjoy and that reflects His perfect will for your life. If you are already doing it, then you know how fulfilling it is. If not, then pray and trust God to lead you into it. He will always help you do His will.

STEP OUT

Peter was in a boat with the other disciples when they saw Jesus walking toward them on the water. Peter wanted to walk on water too, so he asked Jesus to ask him to come. As soon as He did, Peter climbed out of the boat, and he did indeed walk on the water for a short period of time. But then he noticed the wind and began to sink. Jesus reached out, took him by the hand to save him from drowning, and asked him why he was afraid (Matthew 14:22–33). I wonder if the other disciples also wanted to walk on water but were too afraid to leave the safety of the boat.

Many of us live that way. We watch other people coura- geously step out into new things, but we choose safety over adventure. If you truly want to know God's will, you may have to step out of your com- fort zone and try a few things before you find the thing that fits you just right. Being out of God's will is like wearing

> *Being out of God's will is like wearing clothing that is very uncomfortable.*

clothing that is very uncomfortable, but when we are liv- ing in God's will, we are comfortable. Peter walked on water until he looked around and saw the effects of the wind, and we can learn from his actions. If we focus too much on our circumstances instead of following the Holy Spirit, most of us will be too afraid to do anything.

As we age, God's will for us changes, but with proper discernment we will be able to always make the changes graciously. Perhaps it is in the latter years of your life that you will have the time to do what has been in your heart all along.

How do you know when the time has come to stop doing one thing and start doing something else? I will use an example from my own life that I think will help bring understanding. I have made sixty-seven mission trips outside the United States. For many years I traveled overseas to places like India and other parts of Asia, Africa, Australia, Europe, and South America. I went to India more than anywhere else, and I loved being there. We held conferences there and hosted a variety of programs geared toward helping the poor. These trips were very fulfilling, and we always had great favor in these countries.

> *How do you know when the time has come to stop doing one thing and start doing something else?*

When the favor toward our ministry seemed to be decreasing and doors were closing to us, I couldn't understand what was happening. Eventually I was banned from even going into India because a high government official decided they didn't like my bringing the gospel of Christ to the nation, so they put me on a list of people not allowed into the country.

We had similar difficulties arise in other countries. In Cambodia, we had everything set up for a conference, and at the last minute the power to the building we were using was shut off. In addition to this opposition, I began to notice that the trips were harder on me physically and that recovering from them after I returned home took me longer than it once did. Before long, I began losing my desire to take the trips. Desire is one way we can discern God's will.

Why would I suddenly lose my desire to do something I had enjoyed so much for many years? Simply because it was going to be best for me not to drain my energy doing those trips and use it instead for other ministry endeavors, such as television. I cannot physically get into the nation of India, but I am all over India daily on television, broadcasting in about sixty different languages. The government doesn't want me in India, but God does. And nobody can keep me out as long as television and the Internet exist.

I know other people my age who travel to these countries regularly and they say that they are not bothered by the jet lag and that it does not tire them out. This tells me that God wants them to make the trips they make, and it is useless for me to compare myself with them. All I need to do is what God wants me to do; that's all any one of us is responsible to do.

Because I had done overseas ministry in person for many years, it didn't even occur to me for quite a while that God was telling me the season for doing it was over for me. Thankfully, I finally realized there was no longer grace on that particular type of ministry, and I let it go. Joyce Meyer Ministries sends people around the world often, but they go without me. Sometimes I do miss going on those trips, but I know I cannot go and still be strong enough to do the things

I am currently doing. Perhaps someday God will allow me to travel and minister internationally in person again, but for now, He has made it clear to me that my place is in the United States.

GOD MAKES A WAY

When God wants us to do something specific, He always makes a way for us to do it. He provides everything we need—from desire to strength and from energy to finances. But when He wants us to stop doing it, He closes the way. We may still try to force it to work, but we will labor in vain and may become frustrated because it will not produce fruit equivalent to the effort we exert.

> *When God wants us to do something specific, He always makes a way for us to do it.*

I really want you to understand that as you age things will have to change, but these changes can be good if you view them properly. Instead of looking at the foreign mission trips as opportunities I had lost, I was able to look at the sixty-seven opportunities God had given me to travel and minister and at all the good fruit from those trips. My soul misses being able to go, but I have peace in my spirit about not going. When we learn to discern what God is giving us grace to do and what we do not have His grace to do, we can save ourselves much difficulty.

If you are facing some of the things I have been writing about, the first step toward change is facing the reality of where you are at this point in your life. When you hear yourself complaining about all you have to do or even saying, "I just can't keep doing this," it is a sign that something needs to change. You may not be the only one who needs to face reality and be willing to make changes. Your staff, coworkers, family, and other people you are involved with will need to make adjustments, too. In my case, I stopped going on mission trips and delegated other responsibilities to various people at Joyce Meyer Ministries.

There were things I thought that only I could do, and my staff felt the same way, but we all found out that God can move His grace from one person to another for a particular task, and when He does, it works just as well as, or maybe even better than, before. As long as I kept saying yes to other people's desires for my time, I could not make the changes God wanted

> *When you hear yourself complaining about all you have to do, it is a sign that something needs to change.*

me to make. I discovered that the people who truly cared about me understood when I began saying no to some things and even encouraged me to do so. Don't wear yourself out doing things that God is finished with just to please people. He wants you to let go of those things and focus on what He has for you today.

"I HAVE LESS STAMINA NOW THAN
I ONCE HAD. IN A WAY, THIS IS
A GREAT THING. IT'S MADE ME MORE
GRACIOUS AND KIND TO MYSELF.
I'VE ALSO BECOME BETTER AT
SETTING BOUNDARIES, BUT SOFTER
AND GENTLER AT COMMUNICATING
THEM AND SAYING NO WHEN NEEDED.
BEST OF ALL, I'M COMFORTABLE
WITH THE REALITY THAT SOMETIMES
I JUST NEED AN AFTERNOON NAP.
THE DAILY AFTERNOON QUIET TIMES
MY MOM INSISTED ON WHEN I WAS
A CHILD HAVE CIRCLED BACK
AROUND TO BECOMING, AT LONG
LAST, TREASURED GIFTS."

—

M.J.

CHAPTER 11

LEARNING HOW TO REST

Come to me, all you who are weary and burdened, and I will give you rest.

Matthew 11:28

Jesus says in Matthew 11:28 that there will be times when we are weary and burdened, or tired. In those times, He tells us to come to Him and He will give us rest. Jesus offers us rest, but we must be willing to receive it. The psalmist David says:

The Lord is my shepherd; I shall not want. He makes me to lie down in green pastures; He leads me beside the still waters. He restores my soul; He leads me in the paths of righteousness for His name's sake.

Psalm 23:1–3 NKJV

I am a big fan of working hard, and I believe it is godly to do so. But if we don't also have periods of rest, working excessively can be harmful to our health. God said to work six days and rest one day, so we are obviously intended to work more than we rest, but if we don't maintain balanced schedules, we create opportunities for trouble.

I remember reading the life story of a minister who lived in the 1800s and worked very hard, preaching and traveling constantly. His story mentioned that at one time he took a break for three years. I remember wondering why he did that. Although the story did not give a reason, he may have done it because he had worn himself out. It seems that ministry and burnout often go hand in hand. Some ministers are not quick to tell their stories because we often feel we need to be strong all the time and not admit to any weakness, but I have heard enough stories that I know that burnout and exhaustion affect more than a few people in ministry. I think the passion to help people mixed with the responsibility we feel drives us to push beyond the constraints of wisdom.

> *If we don't maintain balanced schedules, we create opportunities for trouble.*

Burnout also affects many people who own businesses or hold jobs with high levels of responsibility. When you know many people are depending on you, you know you need to work, and not working is difficult. Research by the US Travel Association found that in 2018, American workers left 768 million vacation days unused, up 9 percent from 2017. And one-third of those vacation days were forfeited completely, a loss of $65 billion in benefits.

A mom can experience exhaustion and burnout if she has several children, because she will struggle to find time to relax. With preparing meals, doing laundry, keeping up with the children's school projects and activities, and being a chauffeur for all their activities, she rarely has any free time. In addition, many moms homeschool their children, which is a full-time job all by itself.

Anyone can experience burnout unless they use wisdom in managing life's demands. If we want time to relax, we have to schedule it rather than simply wait for it to appear on our calendars. My son and his wife have four young boys, and they schedule a date day or evening once a week. They get a babysitter and spend time together, because doing so is good for their marriage and allows them quiet time.

Just remember that if you don't like your schedule, you are the one who made it, and you are the only one who can change it. Maybe it's time for you to be led by the Holy Spirit and take control of your life rather than simply allowing circumstances and other people's demands to control it. Maybe you need to schedule

> *Just remember that if you don't like your schedule, you are the one who made it, and you are the only one who can change it.*

rest time or fun time on a regular basis and stick to it as you would a very important appointment.

When I received the diagnosis of adrenal fatigue and was

told to rest for eighteen months and only do what I absolutely had to do, my first question to the doctor was, "What
do people *do* when they rest?" My question was pretty funny,
now that I look back on it. No wonder I had a problem! I
didn't understand that sometimes we simply don't need to do
anything that even resembles work for a period of time so we
can recover physically, mentally, and emotionally from all the
work we have already done.

My prescription for eighteen months of rest was necessary because I had gone years without resting properly. The
lack of rest had damaged my entire system to the point that it
could not be healed in a few days. Serious adrenal fatigue can
take eighteen months to two years to recover from, and some
people never recover completely. I understand that, but I also
believe that with God all things are possible, and I know that
He redeems our mistakes and restores our souls and our bodies. I'm trusting God and believing for full recovery, and if
you have worn yourself out, you can trust God to restore all
you have lost, too.

In the early days of my recovery, I was so tired that I
couldn't do much but sit in a recliner and look out the window. But inside, I kept thinking, *I should be doing something*. I
needed to learn to value rest as much as I value work. Maybe
you do, too. There is nothing wrong with you if you need
to rest, and taking time to rest isn't something you should
feel guilty about. Stephen Covey says, "People expect us
to be busy, overworked. It's become a status symbol in our
society—if we're busy, we're important; if we're not busy,
we're almost embarrassed to admit it."

In our accomplishment-driven society, we often think we must justify taking a day off, but God commanded it; therefore, it must be a good thing. If one day of rest out of seven days is what even a young person needs, I think it might be permissible for someone who is seventy or eighty to take off more than one day each week if needed. In addition to taking days off, I have also found that working fewer hours each day

> *There is nothing wrong with you if you need to rest.*

is helpful to me. This type of schedule allows me to still feel productive while not pressing past the point of doing what I can do with God's grace.

When Dave is tired, he rests. It is as simple as that. And if he were to be tired for several days in a row, he would rest for several days in a row. He would not feel guilty or try to figure out what was wrong with him; he would simply rest. The result is that he feels well 99.9 percent of the time. Usually, if I am tired, my first response is to try to figure out why instead of merely accepting my condition and resting, but thank God I am learning and getting better at it all the time.

I remember, when I was very young in ministry, talking with a man who had a large and successful ministry organization. He mentioned (actually bragged) that he had not taken a day off in twelve years. I remember thinking at the time, *How spiritual he must be!* Now I know that he was being unwise, and his pride in not taking a day off in twelve years shows us how wrong our thinking can be. Surely there are many things we can be proud of other than working so hard that we make ourselves sick. When I hear people talk excessively about how hard they work and about everything they are doing all the time, I recognize that they are people who find their worth and value in what they do. They still need to learn that their value lies in being children of God apart from their works.

Sometimes when I share with people that my doctor prescribed eighteen months of rest for me, they respond as I did. They don't know how to rest. They, too, want to know what to do while they rest. The point isn't that we need to sit and do absolutely nothing in order to be resting, but that we need to do something that is relaxing and enjoyable. It can be anything that isn't work related. Different things bring refreshment to different people, and each of us needs to find our own pathway to get the result we need.

I recall a friend telling me that her husband is energized when he is around lots of people. She, on the other hand, says, "They wear me out!" Some find being outdoors very refreshing, while others rest by sitting in their favorite chair in a quiet and beautiful place. I love my home. It is decorated to suit me, and I think it is very pretty, so sitting at home makes me feel comfortable and rested. I love nothing better than my fireplace on a cold day, my recliner, a lightweight blanket, and a good book or movie. I also have a friend who would be refreshed by doing a five-mile hike. If you don't know how to rest, start being adventurous and try different things until you find something that works for you.

REST IS A STEP OF FAITH

Just as Peter took a step of faith to get out of the boat and walk on the water, resting may require a step of faith for many of us. We need to trust God to help us accomplish in six days what we think we need seven days to do. This is similar to the principle of tithing. God can make 90 percent of our money go farther than 100 percent if we will—in faith—give Him the first 10 percent of all of our income.

Until I wrote this book, I never viewed resting as being, in a sense, the same as tithing. But it is. If we honor the principle of the Sabbath, God can multiply our time and fruitfulness.

I don't believe your day of rest needs to be any specific day. You can choose one day and rest the same day every week, or you can alter the day to fit your schedule. But one day out of seven belongs to the Lord. It is His gift to you, and honoring the Sabbath rest will help you manage the other six days better.

Honoring the Sabbath is one of the Ten Commandments. Although we as New Testament believers are no longer subject to the ceremonial Mosaic Law, we are responsible for keeping its moral commands; they have not changed. We would not say it is permissible to murder, lie, or steal because we now live under the New Covenant, so why should we think we no longer need to rest? All of God's commands are for our good, and the Sabbath was made for people, not people for the Sabbath. Honoring the Sabbath is not a rule we keep, but a privilege we enjoy. Take the step of faith and start adding rest to your calendar just as you add other commitments to it. I assure you that God will help you accomplish all you need to do.

INTERNAL REST

The twenty-third Psalm teaches us that God restores our soul as we rest. Our soul is the internal part of us, a part no one sees, but one we are very aware of. A person's soul is composed of the mind, the will, and the emotions. Sometimes we need internal rest (rest in our souls) even more than we need external rest (rest in our bodies). A person can lie on a beach all day and still worry or be angry. If that is the case, the person is not truly resting.

I read somewhere that eight hours of worry is equivalent to forty hours of hard work. How many hours in your life have you wasted worrying? I know I wasted too many, and that contributed to the stress that finally took its toll on my body.

> *Eight hours of worry is equivalent to forty hours of hard work.*

Yet we still find all sorts of reasons to worry. We can worry about what people think of us or about our children, our finances, conditions in the world, our health, how to care for elderly loved ones, what will happen to us as we get older, and a thousand other things. After all the time I wasted worrying, I did learn one lesson: Worry is totally useless and does nothing to change our situations, but it does damage our spiritual, mental, emotional, and physical health.

I believe the only way to stop worrying is to fully realize that we cannot solve our own problems. We can do what we know to do, but then we must enter the rest of God and trust Him. The writer of Hebrews says that the Israelites were not able to enter the rest of God because of their unbelief (Hebrews 3:19). People have the same problem today. True rest, especially internal rest, comes from trusting God completely and believing that He is faithful and will never leave us or forsake us (Deuteronomy 31:6).

When facing a challenge or spiritual warfare, Paul writes that we should do "all the crisis demands" and then "stand firmly" in our place (Ephesians 6:13 AMPC). The word translated *stand* in this verse means to abide or rest in God. Do what you can do—what you believe God wants you to do—then leave your problems in His hands. Luke 18:27 says, "What is impossible with man is possible with God."

Let me encourage you to give your emotions a rest by letting go of all negative feelings. Be extremely diligent in letting go of anger, because it is an emotion that especially wears us out. The only way to not be angry is to learn to forgive quickly, just as God forgives us. Showing mercy to others is much easier on us than judging them. So many people are angry these days that it is appalling. I think it is safe to say that we live in an angry world, and I believe that is partly because many people feel hopeless. Thank God we can hope in Him, and when we do, He never disappoints us (Romans 5:5). Hope is the expectation that something good will happen. The world—people who do not know Christ—does not have that hope.

Our worried, hurried lifestyles drain our energy and leave us worn out, but that can change. A special rest is available to us if we will enter into it. In Hebrews 4:1–3, we read that the promise of entering God's rest still stands, and we should be careful not to fall short of reaching it. As believers, we can enter that rest.

I have felt strongly for the past few months that I should strengthen people in faith by encouraging them to remember that all things are possible with God. When we believe this truth, we can live free from the torment of fear. This includes the fear of getting old or the fear of death. God has each of us in the palm of His hand, and He has a plan for us. The date of our exit from this earth has been set, and when it is time to go, it will be glorious. As Paul writes, "To live is Christ and to die is gain" (Philippians 1:21). He even felt hard-pressed to choose between going to heaven and staying on earth:

> I am torn between the two: I desire to depart and be with Christ, which is better by far; but it is more necessary for you that I remain in the body. Convinced of this, I know that I will remain, and I will continue with all of you for your progress and joy in the faith.
>
> Philippians 1:23–25

Hebrews 4:11 teaches us to "make every effort" to enter the rest of God, which includes entering rest regarding aging and death. Many of our other efforts are useless because we are trying to do what only God can do; instead, we should make an effort to enter God's rest each and every day, in every situation.

"SAVE MONEY, AND MANAGE
YOUR RESOURCES WISELY,
NOT SO THAT YOU CAN
HAVE MORE YOURSELF,
BUT SO THAT YOU CAN HELP
AND BLESS OTHERS."

J.F.F.

CHAPTER 12

FEAR OF THE UNKNOWN

Fear is pain arising from the anticipation of evil.

Aristotle

When we think of aging, we look into the future and usually find a lot of questions with no answers. We ask:

- How long will I live?
- Will I outlive my spouse?
- Will I have enough money to take care of myself once I am no longer working and bringing in an income?
- If I am not able to work, what will I do with all of my time?
- What if I become sick or disabled in some way?

However, we don't need to fear or worry about these things because God promises to be our guide even unto death (Psalm 48:14). Walking by faith, by its nature, means that we do not know everything. God's guidance comes one step at a time, so don't despair if you don't see the whole picture of your future right now.

One of the big issues some people struggle with is the fear of being alone. They may have already outlived their spouse and may not have any children, or they may not have taken the time to develop good relationships with the children they do have. Perhaps they don't have any extended family, such as brothers, sisters, or cousins, or have outlived their closest friends. Although these fears are understandable, they are useless. All they do is steal the energy needed to live today, and they do not help tomorrow at all. As Aristotle rightly observed, fear arises from the anticipation of evil.

Based on the Amplified Bible, Classic Edition version of Proverbs 15:15, I refer to such fears as "evil forebodings." This verse says that our days are "made evil" by these "anxious thoughts and forebodings." We can choose to believe that something good will happen to us just as easily as we can believe that something evil will happen. Believing that good things will happen is much easier on us than having a negative outlook.

A friend of mine recently attended a prayer meeting with approximately 1,200 people in attendance and many more participating online. People emailed prayer requests to the meeting from more than one hundred nations of the world.

When the leaders noticed how many requests mentioned being afraid of something, they commented that they had read that fear is one of the biggest struggles people face today. Sensing the guidance of the Holy Spirit, they focused the prayers of the entire evening on coming against fear and asking God to help people overcome it.

I once read that in most cases, fearing something is usually much worse than actually having it happen. God always gives us the grace (ability) to handle difficult things as we trust Him, but He doesn't give it to us until we actually need it. If we look into the future and don't trust God, we are looking ahead without grace. But faith causes us to look at the future knowing that grace will come when we need it.

> *Fearing something is usually much worse than actually having it happen.*

I heard a story about a young minister who was in prison with an elderly minister. They were both to be burned at the stake the next morning for proclaiming their faith in Jesus. The young man was visibly upset, but the elderly man was very peaceful. The young man struck a match to light a candle and burned his finger. With a great deal of emotion he asked how he could possibly bear being burned at the stake if burning a finger hurt so much. The elderly minister wisely told him that God didn't give him grace to burn his finger, but that as His servant He would give him grace to be burned at the stake when the next morning dawned.

None of us knows what the future will hold, but through faith, as the old saying goes, we do know who holds the future. I'm expecting good things, but if trouble comes, I know that God will strengthen me and give me the grace (power and ability) to handle it.

THE BEAUTY OF TRUSTING GOD

I was talking with someone this morning about how easy life becomes when we finally learn to trust God and believe that He will take care of us. Everything doesn't always go exactly the way we want it to, but God does work out all things for good for those who love Him and want His will (Romans 8:28).

I have finally come to realize that when I have a problem I cannot solve, I can release it to God through prayer and be at peace while He works out the situation. Reaching that point did take me a number of years, so don't feel bad if you are not there yet. The more experience you have with God and the more you see His faithfulness, the easier releasing your anxieties and fears to Him becomes.

For anyone, but especially those in life's latter years, being able to pray instead of worry is a tremendous blessing, because God definitely answers prayer. He does things that we cannot do, and we get to enjoy the victory. God always makes a way for those who trust Him.

Worry robs the power you need to live today because it often operates in the past or the future, neither of which you can do anything about. Think about it: How many times do people worry about what *will* happen or the consequences of what *has* happened? I don't have a statistic, but I think it's a *lot*! Of course, people also worry about what is happening in the present, and that robs them of the power to live and enjoy the day they have.

Worry can even do damage to your body. It is known to give people ulcers and a variety of stomach disturbances. It can also cause colon problems, headaches, nervous tension, and irritability. Even cancer has been linked to the stress of worry. If you have physical impairments, I encourage you to live one day at a time and not waste today worrying about tomorrow.

I recently saw a cartoon with a caption that gave me a good laugh. It said, "When you are past forty and they tell you to put a Band-Aid on what hurts, this is what you look like." The picture inside showed a man with one huge Band-Aid covering his entire body, head to toe.

The cartoon, of course, is an exaggeration, but as we age, we may have days when we feel that everything hurts. I am stiffer than I once was, especially in the mornings, so I have a stretching routine I do each morning that takes about fifteen minutes. This helps relieve the stiffness and helps me manage some back pain I have. Proper stretching exercises are important, especially as we age. Before you start a stretching routine, I recommend seeking medical advice on how to stretch properly, because if you stretch tight muscles too quickly, you can hurt yourself.

Some days, it seems that my body gets up and my brain stays in bed, and it takes a while for me to feel alert. I remember years when I could jump out of bed and begin making decisions and doing all kinds of things, but now I need a little more time to get my body and mind to cooperate with me.

At one time I allowed physical challenges such as these to make me think, *I'm getting old!* However, I don't do that any longer; I simply realize they are part of the aging process and do all I can to combat the symptoms. I

> *Some days, it seems that my body gets up and my brain stays in bed.*

asked my physical trainer, "If I live to be ninety and am still doing the same workout I am doing today, will I still be able to lift the same amount of weight?"

With no hesitation at all, he said, "No," and he went on to explain that our bodies age, and it is just part of life. He assured me that I am in good enough condition from previous years of working out that I will still be able to work out in the future, just not at the same level I do now.

Give yourself permission to change as you age without feeling that it makes you old or weak and feeble.

DEALING WITH DOUBT AND UNCERTAINTY

As we age, we will need to make many important decisions. We will have to decide how long to keep working before we retire. We may realize we no longer need the large home we lived in when our children were growing up and have to decide whether to sell it. If we sell, we'll need to decide whether to move to something smaller or more accessible, perhaps a condo, an apartment, or even a retirement home where we can have access to activities and to other people in the same season of life. If you have children who love you, they can help you with many of these decisions, but ultimately only you can decide what you want and what is best for you.

Making a decision and then doubting it or wondering whether you made the right one is not uncommon. Doubt is actually a form of fear, and it can introduce much confusion into a situation. Have you ever thought, *Did I make the right decision? I don't know. Maybe I did. Well, maybe I didn't.*

We can go back and forth in our heads forever, but I've found that when I'm confused, the best course of action is to stop, turn off my brain, and just look at what's in my heart—not to find out what I *think* I should do, but what I *believe* I should do.

Any decision, especially an important one, deserves a reasonable amount of time for us to pray and ponder the best option. But eventually we will have to make a decision and move forward. Fear is designed by the devil to keep us from moving forward. He uses it to either drive us backward or keep us stuck in one place. Faith is God's gift to those who believe, and with faith we can conquer and overcome fear. Here is a scripture that I clung to for many years while I was in the process of letting God help me face fear and defeat it.

> I sought (inquired of) the Lord and required Him [of necessity and on the authority of His Word], and He heard me, and delivered me from all my fears.
>
> Psalm 34:4 AMPC

I ask you: What are you afraid of today? Are you afraid of getting old? Don't forget that you can age without getting old, but aging is something that happens to all of us. There is no way you can stop it, so there is no need to fear it. With faith in God you will be ready for anything you need to do when the time comes. You have His promise that He will never fail or forsake you, and He will always provide for you.

> He [God] Himself has said, I will not in any way fail you nor give you up nor leave you without support. [I will] not, [I will] not, [I will] not in any degree leave you helpless nor forsake nor let [you] down (relax My hold on you)! [Assuredly not!]
>
> So we take comfort and are encouraged and confidently and boldly say, The Lord is my Helper; I will not be seized with alarm [I will not fear or dread or be terrified].
>
> Hebrews 13:5–6 AMPC

This scripture is so encouraging, and you can go to it anytime you feel afraid concerning the unknown future.

DON'T DREAD GETTING OLDER

Falling into the trap of dreading getting older is easy to do, because we know there will be things we do now that we won't be able to do then. It may be a sport, a hobby, some type of work, or any number of activities. Dread doesn't prevent anything from taking place; it only steals the time we have now. I want to share with you two words that will help you enjoy each day more: *Don't dread*. Dread is simply expecting to have an unpleasant experience. Like fear, it is the opposite of hope and faith.

God doesn't want you to fear or dread anything. It will only steal your joy and your strength to accomplish what you need to do. Being free from

> *Dread doesn't prevent anything from taking place; it only steals the time we have now.*

fear and dread doesn't mean that you will never feel them; it simply means you won't let them control your decisions. I have written an entire book on this, called *Do It Afraid*, specifically to help people break free from having fear control the decisions they make.

Always remember that your attitude toward every situation determines whether you will enjoy it or not. Your attitude belongs to you, and no one can make you have a bad one if you don't want to.

"I WISH SOMEONE HAD TOLD ME
MORE ABOUT THE PHYSICAL
AND HORMONAL CHANGES THAT
COME WITH AGING, NOT SIMPLY
IN A 'BE GRATEFUL YOU ARE
NOT MY AGE,' SORT OF WAY,
BUT WITH A WILLINGNESS
TO SHARE WISDOM, HONEST
COMMUNICATION, AND CARE."

—

M.J.

CHAPTER 13

LISTEN TO YOUR BODY

If you listen to your body when it whispers, you won't have to listen to it scream.

Author Unknown

A doctor once told me that my mind was stronger than my body. He went on to say that my mind was getting me in trouble concerning my health, because even when my body told me to rest, my mind told me I could press through and keep going. At the time I thought that was something to be proud of, but I realize now that it was unwise for me not to listen to my body, and it is unwise for you not to listen to yours.

I believe our bodies often warn us when something is going wrong physically or when we need to pay attention to them. Pain is one of those warning signs. At first, pain whispers that something may be wrong, but if we ignore it long

enough, it eventually screams loud enough that we are forced
to listen.

I speak with many people who tell me about their physical ailments, but when I ask if they have been to the doctor,
they have not. Some say they don't like doctors, or they don't
trust doctors, and some even admit they are afraid of what
their diagnosis may be. All of these reasons are foolish. Problems don't go away just because
people ignore them.

At first, pain whispers that something may be wrong, but if we ignore it long enough, it eventually screams.

I mentioned earlier that I had
breast cancer but didn't need
chemotherapy or radiation treat-
ments because the tumor was
very small when it was found. It
was found early because I had regular mammograms. Thousands of women put off the unpleasant experience of regular
mammograms and later find they have a severe problem. It is
always best to be proactive in dealing with our health so we
will not have to react to an emergency health crisis later.

You might say, "I'm trusting God instead of doctors." If
so, I understand. I spoke the same words for a long time.
But what if God gave us doctors as a gift? I believe all healing
comes from God. It may come miraculously, but it may also
come through medical technology and expertise that God has
given to help us heal.

I read a book by a well-known man of God who suffered
with depression for years. Finally, he began taking medication for his condition. His doctor had been asking him to try

the medication for a long time, but he kept refusing because he was trusting God to heal him. The medicine greatly helped him, and within a short period of time he no longer suffered with depression. He said that he learned to thank God every morning when he took his little white pill and considered it his miracle from God.

Jesus is our Healer. I always advocate going to God before going to anyone else for help and asking Him to heal us and guide us to handle our situations with wisdom. I also believe that all healing comes from God and that He gives medical professionals the brilliance they have. God heals, He does miracles, and He works through doctors and medical technology. If you really believe that God doesn't want you to go to the doctor, be sure you are not simply procrastinating and that your refusal to go isn't based on pride, stubbornness, or fear of a diagnosis you don't want.

BE WISE

If we attend to problems when they are small, we often avoid having to deal with huge problems later. To do so is to use wisdom. Wisdom is one of the greatest gifts that God has given us; it is the accurate use of knowledge. I like to say, "Wisdom is doing now what you will be happy with later."

When Dave was in his mid to late forties, I noticed that he wasn't eating dinner. When I questioned him about it, he said that he felt he was a little bit heavy for his age, so he cut back on his eating until he lost fifteen pounds. I didn't think he was too heavy or large, but he sensed in his heart he would feel better if he wasn't carrying quite as much weight, and he took action. Just recently, I heard him say that he plans to reduce the amount of weight he lifts in the gym because he feels that the heavy weights he has been lifting are not good for him any longer. He is a man who listens to his body, and because of that and God's grace, he stays exceptionally healthy.

Several years ago, Dave began to feel shaky inside or nervous at times, and he hated it. He is a man motivated by peace, so feeling nervous was especially difficult for him. He eventually realized that he felt jittery after drinking caffeine or eating sugar. He has a family history of diabetes, so he went to the doctor but found he had no blood sugar problems. The doctor didn't have an answer as to why sugar was bothering him but did suggest that he could simply be developing a sensitivity to it for some reason.

Most people who drink caffeine don't want to give it up, and most of us don't want to avoid sweets, either. But after a couple of years of experiencing the same symptoms again and again, Dave made a decision. He said, "It is not worth it to keep making myself feel this way, so I'm not going to eat sweets anymore." He can have a little caffeine occasionally, but he stays away from all sugar. I wonder how many people reading this book keep having the same problem over and over, but won't deal with the issue causing it?

Wisdom sees what needs to be done and does it. If you don't get enough sleep, the answer is to go to bed earlier. If you have too much stress in your life, the answer is to cut some things out of your schedule so you are not so busy. If you eat too much sugar, then reduce it. Quite often, the answers to our big problems are simple if we will only do what we know we need to do. The younger we are when we begin applying wisdom to our lives, the better we will feel as we age. We simply cannot abuse our bodies and expect to feel well!

The Book of Proverbs is filled with wisdom. It contains simple, practical answers to everyday problems. For example, Proverbs frequently mentions discipline. If we want to feel well physically, we will certainly need to use discipline in many areas of our lives.

> *Wisdom sees what needs to be done and does it.*

Discipline must be applied to our eating, sleeping, exercising, working, worrying, the way we manage anger, and many other areas of our lives. When applied regularly, discipline brings wonderful results.

There are diseases and other physical problems that we may contract through no fault of our own, but if we can do something to help ourselves be healthy and feel good, then by all means we should do it.

I KNOW I SHOULDN'T DO THIS, BUT...

Do you hear yourself or others say, "I know I shouldn't do this...," but they go ahead and do it anyway? This statement reveals a lot if we really think about it. It means we know what is right, but we choose to do the wrong thing anyway and hope we don't experience any bad results.

The main lesson I learn from studying Proverbs is this: Everything we do has some aftereffect. If we choose good, the results are good; and if we choose poorly, the results are not good! The Book of Proverbs continually speaks of the wise person and the foolish person and tells us how both fare. They have the same choices, but the quality of their lives depends on the decisions they make.

> One who is wise is cautious and turns away from evil,
> but a fool is reckless and careless.
>
> Proverbs 14:16 ESV

Paul writes in his letter to the Ephesians that we are to be careful how we live. He urges us to behave as the wise, not the unwise, and says not to be foolish (Ephesians 5:15–17). The apostle James teaches us that to know what is right to do and then not do it is to sin (James 4:17).

If you know of changes you need to make in order to take better care of your health, then now is the time to act. No matter what decade of your life you are in, whether you're twenty or eighty, you can still help yourself by making wise choices. The earlier you make good choices, the fewer problems you will have in life, but it is never too late to begin.

HONOR GOD IN YOUR BODY

Do you not know that your bodies are temples of the Holy Spirit, who is in you, whom you have received

from God? You are not your own; you were bought at
a price. Therefore honor God with your bodies.

1 Corinthians 6:19–20

I believe that taking good care of our health is one way
we honor God with our bodies. We are the earthly dwelling
places of God's Spirit, and we certainly want to take good care
of His home.

We all age, but we don't have to get old. We can be like
Moses, who, at 120 years of age when he died, still had good
eyesight and was still strong (Deuteronomy 34:7). People
lived longer in Moses' time than they do today, but wanting to be strong for all the days of your life is a good goal. If
you have already damaged your body through poor choices,
regaining your health may take a long time, but you can
do your best to cooperate with God's restoration plan for
your life.

I am pleased when I realize that after all I have been
through in my life, at seventy-eight years young I am sitting
here writing this book, which will hopefully help you take
better care of yourself than I did. I always say my greatest tes-
timony is, "I'm still here." I feel much better today than I did
three years ago, and I continue to make progress all the time.

If you were to ask me what I believe I am doing now that
helps me most on a practical level, I would say taking time
to rest regularly, not eating excessively, taking my vitamins,
getting eight to nine hours of sleep each night because that
is the amount I need, exercising regularly, saying no when I

need to, drinking a lot of water, taking the medicine my body needs, and continuing to help others. I have people to love and a purpose for living, and I am still in pursuit of God's dream for my life.

People frequently ask me when I am going to retire, or if I have any plans for retirement. I can honestly say that I have no plans for retirement. As long as God gives me the grace to carry on, I don't think my age matters to anyone, and it certainly doesn't matter to me.

Staying spiritually strong is as important to our well-being as staying physically strong. I spend regular time with God, study His Word daily, love Him with all the strength I have, and desire to please Him in all that I do. I place great importance on loving people, because I believe that it is very important to our Lord. In addition, I especially like to help people who are in need. It gives me joy, and the joy of the Lord is our strength (Nehemiah 8:10).

"My father, born in 1913, told me this about aging: 'Keep trying to do things that challenge you, and always include younger people among your friends.' More than one hundred years later, this is still wonderful advice."

—

L.M.B.

CHAPTER 14

IT'S NEVER TOO LATE TO DO SOMETHING GREAT

You are never too old to set a new goal or dream a new dream.

C. S. Lewis

One of the most defeating thoughts we can think is that we are too old to start something new. Instead of thinking, *I'm too old to start that now,* you can think, *Now that I have more time, I can finally do the things I've always wanted to do.*

I started Joyce Meyer Ministries when I was forty-two years old and didn't go on television until I was fifty. I never thought I was too old, so I wasn't. There are a lot of people who did great things later in life.

Vera Wang, the famous designer, started out as a figure skater at the age of seven, with dreams of making the Olympic team. But by the time she was a teenager, she realized she would not be able to achieve the level of success required to be a champion. I think it takes great courage to move on and be open to new experiences. She decided to move on to a fashion career and went to school in Paris. While working as a salesperson at Yves Saint Laurent, she met the fashion director at *Vogue* magazine, was offered a job, and invested almost twenty years at *Vogue* magazine. She later became a design director for Ralph Lauren, then opened a bridal shop, and finally launched her own company. She has been extremely successful.

It is important to accept it when we can't do something, as Vera Wang did. Otherwise we can spend our lives being mediocre at something rather than finding out what we can do with excellence. Vera has said that each time she made a move it was very painful, but because she didn't feel that she had reached the summit of her career, she continued searching for her destiny. She realized that not trying was worse than failing.

Very often the journey we take is what gives us the experience we need for what we finally do with our lives. Prior to feeling called to teach God's Word, I was a waitress, a bookkeeper, an office manager, a credit manager, and a stay-at-home mom.

> *The journey we take is what gives us the experience we need for what we finally do with our lives.*

Perhaps there has always been something that you wanted to do in your heart, but you never had the opportunity or never took the risk. Or God may have something for you that is a total surprise, as He did for me. Either way, don't ever be afraid that it is too late to do something great.

At the same time, let me encourage you not to feel that you *have* to do something great later in life. If you want to rest, travel, and enjoy life, that is fine, too. The point I want to make is that it is important not to let your age be the defining factor in your decision-making. I have found myself thinking at times when I have new ideas, *It's a little late in my life to be launching something big.* But then I remember Caleb, who asked God to give him a mountain when he was eighty-five years old (Joshua 14:10–15).

Some believe that Ray Kroc, the founder of McDonald's restaurants, was an overnight success, but he said his success was thirty years in the making. He started McDonald's when he was fifty-two years old, but he had been working for thirty years prior to that as a Red Cross ambulance driver, a piano player, a paper cup salesman, and a Multimixer salesman. As part of his travels for work, he visited a San Bernardino, California, restaurant that had purchased several Multimixers from him. On that trip, he met the McDonald brothers, who had a successful small restaurant with a limited menu featuring hamburgers, french fries, and beverages. In 1955, he bought the rights to the McDonald's name, and by 1958 McDonald's had sold its 100 millionth hamburger.

Colonel Sanders, of Kentucky Fried Chicken fame, also did something remarkable when he was older. Here is his story from Biography.com:

Harland David Sanders was born on September 9, 1890, in Henryville, Indiana. After his father died when he was 6 years old, Sanders became responsible for feeding and taking care of his younger brother and sister. Beginning at an early age, he held down numerous jobs, including farmer, streetcar conductor, railroad fireman and insurance salesman.

At age 40, Sanders was running a service station in Kentucky, where he would also feed hungry travelers. Sanders eventually moved his operation to a restaurant across the street and featured a fried chicken so notable that he was named a Kentucky colonel in 1935 by Governor Ruby Laffoon.

In 1952, Sanders began franchising his chicken business. His first franchise sale went to Pete Harman, who ran a restaurant in Salt Lake City where "Kentucky Fried Chicken" had the allure of a Southern regional specialty. When a new interstate reduced traffic at Sanders' own restaurant in North Carolina, he sold the location in 1955. He then [at age 65], started traveling across the country, cooking batches of chicken from restaurant to restaurant, striking deals that paid him a nickel for every chicken the restaurant sold. In 1964, with more than 600 franchised outlets, he sold his interest in the company for $2 million to a group of investors.

The famous chef Julia Child was forty-nine years of age

when she and two other women published *Mastering the Art of French Cooking*, which launched her career.

Susan Boyle, the amazing singer, was discovered at age forty-seven on the *Britain's Got Talent* television show. She was an unemployed charity worker who lived alone with her cat, Pebbles, and had never been kissed. When she walked out on the stage to perform, no one thought she would be able to sing well, based on her appearance and her mannerisms. But she shocked everyone when she opened her mouth and out came her amazing voice. Ten years later, she had sold millions of albums and won two Grammy awards.

You may yet surprise people too if you are not afraid to try new things!

DON'T LET PEOPLE DETERMINE YOUR DESTINY

Fred Astaire was a celebrated American dancer, singer, actor, choreographer, and television presenter whose career spanned seventy-six years. At his very first audition, he was told that he couldn't sing, was balding, and could dance *a little*. History is filled with stories such as these—stories of people who seemed insignificant to others but ended up surprising everyone because they didn't stop trying.

Like many others, I was told that I couldn't possibly have a successful ministry. The naysayers said I didn't have the education, that women didn't belong in ministry, and that I didn't have the right personality. They were right. But I did have God, and with God all things are possible! Now, forty-five years after those declarations of doom, I am still going strong for Him.

God chooses and uses the foolish things of the world to confound those who think they are wise. He often takes what the world would discard as useless and uses it for His glory (1 Corinthians 1:27–31). No matter how you may have failed in the past, God can take the fragments of your life and arrange them in such a way that they become something amazing.

If we let what other people think and say about us determine what we will or won't do, most of us won't do much. There are always plenty of people who doubt we will ever amount to much, but "if God is for us, who can be against us?" (Romans 8:31) or stop us from succeeding?

> *If we let what other people think and say about us determine what we will or won't do, most of us won't do much.*

Doing something great doesn't mean you have to do it on a platform or a stage. My son's wife is an amazing woman whose life's dream was to be a wife and a mother. They have four boys under eleven years old. She homeschools them and is a great mom and a great wife. To me, she is amazing, and who knows—she and my son may be raising a future president, an Olympic ski champion, or four great men of God.

I think all of my children are amazing, as I'm sure you do

too, if you have them. However, even more important is that God thinks we are all amazing. Young or old, educated or not, wealthy or poor—God has great plans for all of us.

> However, as it is written: "What no eye has seen, what no ear has heard, and what no human mind has conceived"—the things God has prepared for those who love him.
>
> 1 Corinthians 2:9

God has plans for your life that you cannot even imagine, but you have to believe that all things are possible with Him (Matthew 19:26). You don't have to be especially talented; you just need to love God. He will guide you and enable you to do things in your latter years that others couldn't do even in their youth.

NEVER SAY "NO WAY"

We have a habit of allowing the limitations of our thinking to determine what we can and cannot do. However, when we run out of our human strength, that's when God takes over. I will admit that at the age of seventy-eight, I don't have the natural energy and stamina I once had. I have had to slow down and, naturally, I am not doing as much as I once did. But God is showing me ways to accomplish more with less effort. That is what happens when He blesses something.

Every day of my life, I take the same advice I am giving you in this book. I don't allow myself to lie in bed and dread getting up because I know something in my body may hurt. I refuse to waste time dreaming about the "good old days," but I make the most of the good days I still have. I'm doing my best to take care of myself by exercising, eating right (at least most of the time), getting proper rest, and not worrying or allowing other negative emotions to drain me of the energy I need for living.

When I am confronted with a challenge and hear myself thinking, *There is no way I can do that*, I remember that with God, we are never without a way, because He is "the way" (John 14:6). If I say I can't do something, it is only because I know God doesn't want me to do it; otherwise I keep putting one foot in front of the other and continue to be amazed at what God is doing daily.

When we don't know the way we should go in a certain situation, God can show us a new way—perhaps a way that no one has ever thought of. Our part in seeing the amazing power of God at work is to not give up.

In the Gospel of Luke, we read a story of a man who was too sick to walk being carried on a mat by some friends to see Jesus. They reached the house where Jesus was, but they found *no way* to enter it because of the huge crowd. Instead of giving up and returning home, they went up on the roof, removed some tiles, and lowered the man on his mat into the middle of the crowd right in front of Jesus (Luke 5:17–19). When Jesus saw their faith, He said, "Friend, your sins are forgiven," and He healed the man (Luke 5:20, 24–25).

God is moved by our faith, not our doubt, dread, fear, and unbelief.

One of my favorite Bible stories is about a wealthy tax collector named Zacchaeus. When he heard that Jesus was coming to his town, he wanted to see Him. But Zacchaeus was a man short in stature and could not see over the crowd of people. Instead of saying, "There is no way," and giving up, he looked for a way. He ran ahead of the crowd and climbed a tree so he could see Jesus. He not only saw Jesus; Jesus saw him, too. When Jesus approached the tree, He looked up and told Zacchaeus to come down because He would stay at his house that day (Luke 19:1–6).

This story is amazing because tax collectors were notoriously wicked in New Testament times. People hated them not only because they collected the taxes, but also because they frequently added to the tax in order to keep some money for themselves. Jesus didn't judge Zacchaeus according to his sin, but saw his faith. The people muttered because Jesus went to a sinner's house. But they did not know the whole story, which is often the case when we judge others. Zacchaeus told Jesus he was willing to give half of his possessions to the poor and that if he had cheated anyone, he would repay them four times more than he had taken (Luke 19:7–8). This was Jesus' reply:

Today salvation has come to this house, because this man, too, is a son of Abraham. For the Son of Man came to seek and to save the lost.

Luke 19:9–10

In another gospel story, blind Bartimaeus heard that Jesus was passing near where he was sitting and he began to shout, "Jesus, Son of David, have mercy on me!" The people told him to be quiet, "but he shouted all the more" (Mark 10:46–48). I love what happened next. The Scripture says that Jesus stopped! He called Bartimaeus to Him and healed him (Mark 10:49–52). All the people tried to stop Bartimaeus, but he ignored them and pressed through to his miracle. We can be like Bartimaeus and refuse to think there is no way, regardless of what we face.

HOW DOES OPPOSITION AFFECT YOU?

We all encounter opposition in life, just as Bartimaeus did. We never know when it will come. Just as storms are not always in the weather forecast, neither is opposition. Let me ask you: Does opposition weaken your resolve and discourage or even depress you—or does it make you all the more determined to keep pressing forward?

As we age, we will face different types of opposition. It may be that you gain weight more easily now or that you need more time to recover from physical activity than you did a few years ago. It could be that your body simply doesn't cooperate with you as well

> *Just as storms are not always in the weather forecast, neither is opposition.*

as it once did, and you either need to make adjustments in what you do or to be more determined than ever in order not to give up. Opposition may present itself in the form of losing loved ones or changes in your financial situation, but I can assure you that opposition will come in a variety of ways at various times in life.

Paul said that when a wide door of opportunity opened to him, it came with many adversaries (1 Corinthians 16:9). He seemed to experience opposition almost continually, but he refused to give up.

It is important for us to follow Paul's example and have a steadfast mind. Don't be weary in doing good, because in due season you will reap a harvest if you don't give up (Galatians 6:9). God always provides a way out of your situation, or He gives you extra strength (grace) to bear it graciously.

Your life may not turn out the way you expected it to, but it can be good if you accept it joyfully. Every day won't be perfect, but with the right attitude you can deal with whatever comes graciously. You can age gracefully!

CLOSING COMMENTS

Taking good care of yourself will require discipline, faith, and an investment of your time. I urge you to be an investor, not a gambler. Investors do the right thing now with the hope of future benefits, but gamblers do the wrong thing and hope that it won't cause any problems.

Pray and partner with God in your health. Let the Holy Spirit guide you in the practical aspects of your life as well as the spiritual ones. You are very important to God and to helping build His Kingdom. I would encourage you to think often about His promise in Isaiah 46:4: "Even to your old age and gray hairs, I am he, I am he who will sustain you. I have made you and I will carry you; I will sustain you and I will rescue you."

Remember to rest. Be kind to yourself, and don't feel that you are alive to keep everyone on the planet happy while ignoring your own needs. Don't allow anything you possess or your career to become more important to you than it should be. Always keep God first.

> *Be kind to yourself.*

I commend you to the grace of our Lord Jesus Christ, with the hope that you will live a full, healthy, and fruitful life!

Do you have a real relationship with Jesus?

God loves you! He created you to be a special, unique, one-of-a-kind individual, and He has a specific purpose and plan for your life. And through a personal relationship with your Creator—God—you can discover a way of life that will truly satisfy your soul.

No matter who you are, what you've done, or where you are in your life right now, God's love and grace are greater than your sin— your mistakes. Jesus willingly gave His life so you can receive forgiveness from God and have new life in Him. He's just waiting for you to invite Him to be your Savior and Lord.

If you are ready to commit your life to Jesus and follow Him, all you have to do is ask Him to forgive your sins and give you a fresh start in the life you are meant to live. Begin by praying this prayer . . .

Lord Jesus, thank You for giving Your life
for me and forgiving me of my sins so I can have
a personal relationship with You. I am sincerely
sorry for the mistakes I've made, and I know
I need You to help me live right.

Your Word says in Romans 10:9, "If you declare
with your mouth, 'Jesus is Lord,' and believe in
your heart that God raised him from the dead,
you will be saved" (NIV). I believe You are the Son
of God and confess You as my Savior and Lord.
Take me just as I am, and work in my heart,
making me the person You want me to be.
I want to live for You, Jesus, and I am so grateful
that You are giving me a fresh start in my
new life with You today.

I love You, Jesus!

It's so amazing to know that God loves us so much! He wants to have a deep, intimate relationship with us that grows every day as we spend time with Him in prayer and Bible study. And we want to encourage you in your new life in Christ.

Please visit joycemeyer.org/KnowJesus to request Joyce's book *A New Way of Living*, which is our gift to you. We also have other free resources online to help you make progress in pursuing everything God has for you.

Congratulations on your fresh start in your life in Christ! We hope to hear from you soon.

ABOUT THE AUTHOR

JOYCE MEYER is one of the world's leading practical Bible teachers. A *New York Times* bestselling author, Joyce's books have helped millions of people find hope and restoration through Jesus Christ. Joyce's program, *Enjoying Everyday Life*, airs around the world on television, radio, and the Internet. Through Joyce Meyer Ministries, Joyce teaches internationally on a number of topics with a particular focus on how the Word of God applies to our everyday lives. Her candid communication style allows her to share openly and practically about her experiences so others can apply what she has learned to their lives.

Joyce has authored more than one hundred books, which have been translated into more than one hundred languages, and over 65 million of her books have been distributed worldwide. Bestsellers include *Power Thoughts*; *The Confident Woman*; *Look Great, Feel Great*; *Starting Your Day Right*; *Ending Your Day Right*; *Approval Addiction*; *How to Hear from God*; *Beauty for Ashes*; and *Battlefield of the Mind*.

Joyce's passion to help hurting people is foundational to the vision of Hand of Hope, the missions arm of Joyce Meyer Ministries. Hand of Hope provides worldwide humanitarian outreaches such as feeding programs, medical care, orphanages, disaster response, human trafficking intervention and rehabilitation, and much more—always sharing the love and gospel of Christ.

JOYCE MEYER MINISTRIES

U.S. & FOREIGN OFFICE ADDRESSES

Joyce Meyer Ministries
P.O. Box 655
Fenton, MO 63026
USA
(636) 349-0303

**Joyce Meyer Ministries—
Canada**
P.O. Box 7700
Vancouver, BC V6B 4E2
Canada
(800) 868-1002

**Joyce Meyer Ministries—
Australia**
Locked Bag 77
Mansfield Delivery Centre
Queensland 4122
Australia
(07) 3349 1200

**Joyce Meyer Ministries—
England**
P.O. Box 1549
Windsor SL4 1GT
United Kingdom
01753 831102

**Joyce Meyer Ministries—
South Africa**
P.O. Box 5
Cape Town 8000
South Africa
(27) 21-701-1056

**Joyce Meyer Ministries—
Francophonie**
29 avenue Maurice Chevalier
77330 Ozoir la Ferriere
France

**Joyce Meyer Ministries—
Germany**
Postfach 761001
22060 Hamburg
Germany
+49 (0)40 / 88 88 4 11 11

**Joyce Meyer Ministries—
Netherlands**
Lorenzlaan 14
7002 HB Doetinchem
+31 657 555 9789

**Joyce Meyer Ministries—
Russia**
P.O. Box 789
Moscow 101000
Russia
+7 (495) 727-14-68

OTHER BOOKS BY JOYCE MEYER